HELL
You
Say!

by Carl G. Johnson

TIMOTHY BOOKS
NEWTOWN, PENNSYLVANIA
18940

CONTENTS

PREFACE

Sometime ago I read an article in a Christian magazine that the people of America were buying many books. As they went into the bookstores in this country they were asking for books on different subjects, and I was greatly surprised that among the subjects they were interested in, HELL was named as the first one.

I could not get this out of my mind. I began to pray that God would let me write a book about Hell and make it available to the American public. I shared these thoughts with my friend, Rev. Albert S. Taylor, the President of Hearthstone Publications, Inc., and he very graciously consented to publish a book on this subject and distribute it freely throughout the country.

In study and preparation I found that very little has been written about HELL in this century. I found only a few articles, sermons, and booklets written recently. Leslie H. Woodson, who very recently wrote the book *Hell and Salvation*, comments on this: "Throughout the examination of the concept of hell in the evangelistic mission of the Church, we have been impressed by several things. First is the scarcity of recent or contemporary writing and preaching on the subject. During the first eighteen hundred years of the Christian era the church was almost obsessed with the joys of heaven and the horrors of hell. Since that time interest has waned until, following World War II, hardly anything of serious consequence has been undertaken in the field. One is fortunate to find a paragraph or even a sentence in a theological work or printed sermon which relates directly to the subject of Hell. The investigator is doubly blessed if he discovers a whole

V

chapter or even several pages in any kind of writing. With rare exception, the churchgoer can attend worship for years without hearing a word about Hell. The scarcity of materials gives us our first clue that the subject of Hell is taboo in many quarters and ignored in others." — (*Hell and Salvation*, pp. 103-104).

I read everything I could find on this subject and I am indebted to the writers of the past and present whose materials have been very helpful to me.

In my study I found also that many people do not believe in a literal Hell.

A well-known British preacher, in answer to the questions of a number of young people, made this statement which received front-page publicity some years ago: "I am a bit horrified at the number of young people who send me in questions on what I think about Heaven and Hell. I think it is quite disgraceful for young people to be bothering about Heaven and Hell at their age. It is a form of escapism. Religion is to make them different here and now. They should be following Christ in their daily lives now, and not worrying about Heaven and Hell for themselves or their friends. I am sure there is a Hell on earth. Basically Hell is to be the child of God and be without God. A lost child who desperately wants his father and cannot find him is desperately miserable. That's what Hell is. Whether there is a Hell as a state after death is a question upon which Christians differ."

Universalist Nels Ferre writes, "Eternal Hell is naturally out of question both as sub-justice and sub-love. No human judge has a right to inflict infinite punishment for finite transgression.

"The very conception of an eternal Hell is monstrous and an insult to the conception of last things in other religions, not to mention the Christian doctrine of God's sovereign love. Such a doctrine would either make God a tryant, where any human Hitler would be a third-degree saint, and the concentration camps of human torture, the King's picnic grounds. That such a doctrine could be conceived, not to mention believed, shows how far from any understanding of the love of God many people once were and, alas, still are."

The cults reject the Bible doctrine of Hell. Christian Science teaches that no final judgment awaits man and that Hell fire is the ravings and imaginations of mortal error. Jehovah's Witnesses teach that it is absurd to suppose that God would perpetuate existence forever in torment. They teach that the second death is extinction. Seventh Day Adventists teach that sinners will go to Hell, but that they will be annihilated. (Homer Duncan, *The Lake of Fire*, pp. 1-2).

Colonel R. G. Ingersoll, agnostic, said, "Ladies and Gentlemen: The idea of a hell was born of revenge and brutality on the one side, and cowardice on the other . . . I have no respect for any human being who believes in it. I have no respect for any man who preaches it. . . . I dislike this doctrine, I hate it, I despise it, I defy this doctrine. . . . This doctrine of hell is infamous beyond all power to express."

The well-known novelist, W. Somerset Maugham, stated, "I do not believe in an after-life, so I have no fear of hell fire, and I don't have to face the prospect of eternal boredom in Heaven."

When Irvin S. Cobb, the internationally famous humorist and writer, died in March, 1944, he referred to Heaven as "a powerfully dull place populated to a considerable and uncomfortable degree by prigs, time-servers and unpleasantly aggressive individuals," and then he added that "Hell may have a worse climate but undoubtedly the company is sprightlier." Of course Cobb did not believe in Hell, for he insisted that those in charge of his burial "avoid reading the so-called Christian burial service, which, in view of the language employed in it, I regard as one of the most cruel and paganish things inherited by our forbears from our remote pagan ancestry. Instead, let the 23rd Psalm be read. This has no threat of eternal hell-fire." — (Lehman Strauss, *Life After Death*. pp. 48-49).

In the book, *The Gathering Storm in the Churches*, the results of a questionnaire sent to thousands of Protestant ministers are recorded. The ministers were asked, among other things, about their belief in Hell and the 7,441 clergymen responded in this manner: 58 percent of the Methodists, 60 percent of the Episcopalians, 54 percent of the Presbyterians, and 35 percent of the American Baptists agreed that "Hell does not refer to a special location after death, but to the experience of self-estrangement, guilt, and meaninglessness in this life." In other words, they did not believe in a literal Hell.

Phyllis Batelle, a columnist for the Chicago *Daily News*, wrote a few years ago: "Some people say America is going to hell.

"The phrase falls trippingly and naturally off the tongue but it is a non-thinking man's cliche.

"How could America go to hell? It is an absurd idea, as dated as penny candy and Elsie Dinsmore. The days of brimstone have vanished, and hell is now only a word to be tossed into casual conversation, not a post-mortem geographical area.

"Dr. Ralph Sockman, a Methodist minister, wrote about thirty years ago, 'We have to find a new moral corrective besides hell. People aren't worried about sin any more'."

A recent survey by Dr. George Gallup showed that 68 percent of the American people believe in Heaven but only 54 percent are persuaded of the reality of Hell.

The late Louis Cassels, religion editor for United Press International, saw the difference between the two figures as "a gauge of the great repugnance which the concept of eternal punishment excites in many orthodox Christians." He says that people can't believe that "the loving, merciful, forgiving God revealed by Jesus Christ would consign any poor wretch to a place of perpetual torment."

Another poll of ministerial students at eight leading

VIII

theological schools in America taken by Louis Harris and Associates revealed that 71 percent of them did not believe in a literal Heaven or Hell.

The Chicago *Daily News* recently printed an article concerning a religious survey taken. According to this survey only twelve people out of 100 thought there was any possibility of their going to Hell.

There are other people who make a joke out of Hell. Robert L. Summer wrote about that:

Hell has long been riding high as a number one selection on the jokester "Hit Parade." More jokes are told, perhaps, with the Lake of Fire as their theme than with reference to any other single subject. Usually they'd feature the devil in long, red flannel underwear, cloven hooves, horns and a pitchfork tail. Mingled into the narrative are asbestos suits, Satan giving orders about how fast to shovel coal, and other incidental, colorful sidelights. The stories are usually climaxed with a rib-splitting punchline and followed by gales of laughter. Each one who joins in the ribaldry is subtly saying, consciously or unconsciously, "Yes, I think this business of Hell is just a great big joke! Surely it isn't anything to get seriously alarmed or excited about." But this philosophy is completely false! Hell *is* something to soberly, seriously consider with reference to its reality. (*Hell Is No Joke*, p. 8).

The word is heard in the conversation of many people. A psychiatrist answered the question, "Why is the word 'Hell' used so commonly?" by saying, "Something deep in our subconscious makes us afraid that we may go to Hell, and so we use the word 'Hell' all the time."

A Canadian magazine called *The Northern Lights* contains the following: "One of the latest and boldest moves of the enemy in America has been the plan to build 'Hell Incorporated'." A $40,000 lot has been purchased in Las Vegas, Nevada, where Hell Incorporated is to be built. It is to be run day and night, twenty-four hours every day in the week, and it will contain every kind of amusement and vice that exists. It is said that a large neon sign will advertise the place. It will be built in the form of a devil with an arrow for a pitchfork which constantly moves pointing the way to "Hell." It is also said that between Los Angeles and Las Vegas, large roadside signs will read: "You're on the road to Hell," "This is the road to Hell," "Hell is Fun," and others.

William G. T. Shedd spoke truthfully when he said: "The age which is most reckless of law, and most vicious in practice, is the age that has the loosest conception of penalty and is the most inimical to the doctrine of endless retribution." — (*Doctrine of Endless Punishment*, Chapter 3).

Because of the lack of Biblical teaching on the subject of Hell, many people are confused and bewildered. A book entitled *That Unknown Country* has been written, which is a compilation of the views of men across the centuries concerning Hell. The title aptly describes the place, because so many know so little about it. An editorial in a major newspaper has asked for more preaching on Hell. Winston Churchill once said, "The moral landslide in Great Britain can be traced to the fact that Heaven and Hell are no longer proclaimed throughout the land." Dr. A. C. Dixon said, "If we had more preaching of Hell in the pulpit, we might have less Hell in the community."

In this book I want to share with the readers three things I have learned in my study of Hell:

1. What the Bible Says About Hell.
2. What Men Have Said About Hell.
3. What to Do to Keep Out of Hell.

It is my prayer that you who are already saved from that awful place may, in the words of Dr. R. A. Torrey: "Meditate upon it in its practical, personal bearings, until your heart is burdened by the awful peril of the wicked and you rush out to spend the last dollar, if need be, and the last ounce of strength you have, in saving those imperiled men from the certain, awful hell of conscious agony and shame to which they are fast hurrying." (*What the Bible Teaches*, pp. 313-14).

It is my prayer also that you who are not yet saved may be given a realization of the certainty, reality, and awfulness of Hell and you may "flee from the wrath to come" (Matthew 3:7), and put your complete trust in Jesus Christ as your own personal Lord and Saviour, the One Who will save you "from the wrath to come" (I Thessalonians 1:10).

"But God commendeth his love toward us, in that, while we were yet sinners, Christ died for us. Much more then, being now justified by his blood, we shall be saved from wrath through him" (Romans 5:8,9).

Though there is a Hell for every sinner outside of Christ, thank God, there is Christ for every sinner outside of Hell.

I

WHAT THE BIBLE SAYS ABOUT HELL

In the first part of this book I want to share with you what the Bible says about Hell. Evangelist Hyman Appelman wrote: "I know there is a Hell, not because I was taught the fact in seminary. I know there is a Hell, not because my denomination believes it. I believe there is a Hell, not because my people, the orthodox Jews, have always believed it. I know there is a Hell, not because all orthodox, Fundamental Christians, in all the world, of every persuasion, believe it. That is not enough. Men may be mistaken. The best of them may be wrong. Men may devise a theory which spreads universally but is wrong nevertheless. *I believe that there is a Hell because God says so in His Holy Book.*"

The Bible is the only authoritative source of information concerning Hell, and it says more about Hell than it does about Heaven. Even the infidel Robert Ingersoll said, "The Bible is the foundation of Hell; Hell will never be disposed of till the inspiration of the Bible is."

The English word *hell* is found fifty-four times in the Bible. Here are the references to this word every time it is mentioned in the Bible:

EVERY REFERENCE TO THE WORD "HELL" IN THE BIBLE

Old Testament References — 31 Times

"For a fire is kindled in mine anger, and shall burn unto the lowest *hell*, and shall consume the earth with her increase, and set on fire the foundations of the mountains." (Deuteronomy 32:22).

"The sorrows of *hell* compassed me about; the snares of death prevented me;" (II Samuel 22:6).

"It is as high as heaven; what canst thou do? deeper than *hell*; what canst thou know?" (Job 11:8).

"*Hell* is naked before him, and destruction hath no covering." (Job 26:6).

"The wicked shall be turned into *hell*, and all the nations that forget God." (Psalm 9:17).

"For thou wilt not leave my soul in *hell*; neither wilt thou suffer thine Holy One to see corruption." (Psalm 16:10).

"The sorrows of *hell* compassed me about: the snares of death prevented me." (Psalm 18:5).

"Let death seize upon them, and let them go down quick into *hell*: for wickedness is in their dwellings, and among them." (Psalm 55:15).

"For great is thy mercy toward me: and thou hast delivered my soul from the lowest *hell*." (Psalm 86:13).

"The sorrows of death compassed me, and the pains of *hell* gat hold upon me: I found trouble and sorrow." (Psalm 116:3).

"If I ascend up into heaven, thou are there: if I make my bed in *hell*, behold, thou art there." (Psalm 139:8).

"Her feet go down to death; her steps take hold on *hell*." (Proverbs 5:5).

"Her house is the way to *hell*, going down to the chambers of death." (Proverbs 7:27).

"But he knoweth not that the dead are there; and that

her guests are in the depths of *hell.*" (Proverbs 9:18).
"*Hell* and destruction are before the LORD: how much more then the hearts of the children of men?" (Proverbs 15:11).

"The way of life is above to the wise, that he may depart from *hell* beneath." (Proverbs 15:24).

"Thou shalt beat him with the rod, and shalt deliver his soul from *hell.*" (Proverbs 23:14).

"*Hell* and destruction are never full; so the eyes of man are never satisfied." (Proverbs 27:20).

"Therefore *hell* hath enlarged herself, and opened her mouth without measure: and their glory, and their multitude, and their pomp, and he that rejoiceth, shall descend into it." (Isaiah 5:14).

"*Hell* from beneath is moved for thee to meet thee at thy coming: it stirreth up the dead for thee, even all the chief ones of the earth; it hath raised up from their thrones all the kings of the nations." (Isaiah 14:9).

"Yet thou shalt be brought down to *hell,* to the sides of the pit." (Isaiah 14:15).

"Because ye have said, We have made a covenant with death, and with *hell* are we at agreement; when the overflowing scourge shall pass through, it shall not come unto us: for we have made lies our refuge, and under falsehood have we hid ourselves:" (Isaiah 28:15).

"And your covenant with death shall be disannulled, and your agreement with *hell* shall not stand; when the overflowing scourge shall pass through, then ye shall be trodden down by it." (Isaiah 28:18).

"And thou wentest to the king with ointment, and didst increase thy perfumes, and didst send thy messengers far off, and didst debase thyself even unto *hell.*" (Isaiah ˜57:9).

"I made the nations to shake at the sound of his fall, when I cast him down to *hell* with them that descend into the pit: and all the trees of Eden, the choice and best of Lebanon, all that drink water, shall be comforted in the nether parts of the earth." (Ezekiel 31:16).

3

"They also went down into *hell* with him unto them that be slain with the sword; and they that were his arm, that dwelt under his shadow in the midst of the heathen." (Ezekiel 31:17).

"The strong among the mighty shall speak to him out of the midst of *hell* with them that help him: they are gone down, they lie uncircumcised, slain by the sword." (Ezekiel 32:21).

"And they shall not lie with the mighty that are fallen of the uncircumcised, which are gone down to *hell* with their weapons of war: and they have laid their swords under their heads, but their iniquities shall be upon their bones, though they were the terror of the mighty in the land of the living." (Ezekiel 32:27).

"Though they dig into *hell*, thence shall mine hand take them; though they climb up to heaven, thence will I bring them down:" (Amos 9:2).

"And said, I cried by reason of mine affliction unto the LORD, and he heard me; out of the belly of *hell* cried I, and thou heardest my voice." (Jonah 2:2).

"Yea also, because he transgresseth by wine, he is a proud man, neither keepeth at home, who enlargeth his desire as *hell*, and is as death, and cannot be satisfied, but gathereth unto him all nations, and heapeth unto him all people:" (Habakkuk 2:5).

New Testament References — 23 Times

"But I say unto you, That whosoever is angry with his brother without a cause shall be in danger of the judgment: and whosoever shall say to his brother, Raca, shall be in danger of the council: but whosoever shall say, Thou fool, shall be in danger of *hell* fire." (Matthew 5:22).

"And if thy right eye offend thee, pluck it out, and cast it from thee: for it is profitable for thee that one of thy members should perish, and not that thy whole body should be cast into *hell*." (Matthew 5:29).

"And if thy right hand offend thee, cut it off, and cast it

4

from thee: for it is profitable for thee that one of thy members should perish, and not that thy whole body should be cast into *hell.*" (Matthew 5:30).

"And fear not them which kill the body, but are not able to kill the soul: but rather fear him which is able to destroy both soul and body in *hell.*" (Matthew 10:28).

"And thou, Capernaum, which are exalted unto heaven, shalt be brought down to *hell*: for if the mighty works, which have been done in thee, had been done in Sodom, it would have remained until this day." (Matthew 11:23).

"And I say also unto thee, That thou are Peter, and upon this rock I will build my church; and the gates of *hell* shall not prevail against it." (Matthew 16:18).

"And if thine eye offend thee, pluck it out, and cast it from thee: it is better to enter into life with one eye, rather than having two eyes to be cast into *hell* fire." (Matthew 18:9).

"Woe unto you, scribes and Pharisees, hypocrites! for ye compass sea and land to make one proselyte, and when he is made, ye make him twofold more the child of *hell* than yourselves." (Matthew 23:15).

"Ye serpents, ye generation of vipers, how can ye escape the damnation of *hell*?" (Matthew 23:33).

"And if thy hand offend thee, cut it off: it is better for thee to enter into life maimed, than having two hands to go into *hell*, into the fire that never shall be quenched:" (Mark 9:43).

"And if thy foot offend thee, cut it off: it is better for thee to enter halt into life, than having two feet to be cast into *hell*, into the fire that never shall be quenched:" (Mark 9:45).

"And if thine eye offend thee, pluck it out: it is better for thee to enter into the kingdom of God with one eye, than having two eyes to be cast into *hell* fire:" (Mark 9:47).

"And thou, Capernaum, which are exalted to heaven, shalt be thrust down to *hell.*" (Luke 10:15).

5

"But I will forewarn you whom ye shall fear: Fear him, which after he hath killed hath power to cast into *hell*; yea, I say unto you, Fear him." (Luke 12:5). "And in *hell* he lift up his eyes, being in torments, and seeth Abraham afar of, and Lazarus in his bosom." (Luke 16:23).

"Because thou wilt not leave my soul in *hell*, neither wilt thou suffer thine Hole One to see corruption." (Acts 2:27).

"He seeing this before spake of the resurrection of Christ, that his soul was not left in *hell*, neither his flesh did see corruption." (Acts 2:31).

"And the tongue is a fire, a world of iniquity: so is the tongue among our members, that it defileth the whole body, and setteth on fire the course of nature; and it is set on fire of *hell*." (James 3:6).

"For if God spared not the angels that sinned, but cast them down to *hell*, and delivered them into chains of darkness, to be reserved unto judgment;" (II Peter 2:4).

"I am he that liveth, and was dead; and, behold, I am alive for evermore, Amen; and have the keys of *hell* and of death." (Revelation 1:18).

"And I looked, and behold a pale horse: and his name that sat on him was Death, and *Hell* followed with him. And power was given unto them over the fourth part of the earth, to kill with sword, and with hunger, and with death, and with the beasts of the earth." (Revelation 6:8).

"And the sea gave up the dead which were in it; and death and *hell* delivered up the dead which were in them: and they were judged every man according to their works." (Revelation 20:13).

"And death and *hell* were cast into the lake of fire. This is the second death." (Revelation 20:14).

SHEOL

The Old Testament was written originally in the Hebrew language and the New Testament in the Greek

6

language. The Hebrew word which is translated "*hell*" in the Old Testament is *sheol.* The meaning of *sheol* is "the world of the dead," the hidden world, the unseen world. It denotes the place of departed spirits, including both the saved and the lost. This Hebrew word has various translations. The King James Version of the Bible translates *sheol* in the Old Testament as "hell" thirty-one times, "grave" thirty-one times, and "pit" three times, a total of sixty-five times. This variation produces confusion in the mind of the English reader. The translators of the American Standard Version did not translate the word into English but transliterated it into the English uniformly as *sheol.*

The word for "grave" in the Hebrew is altogether different from the word *sheol.* The Hebrew word for "grave" where the body goes at death is *qeber*, while the place where the spirit goes at death is *sheol.* To show the difference in the two words:

1. The word *sheol* is never used in the plural, but the word for "grave" is used many times in the plural, proving that there are many *graves* but only one *sheol.*

2. We never read in the Bible that anyone has a *sheol,* but we often read of a person having a *grave.*

3. The body is never said to be in *sheol* and the spirit is never said to be in the *grave.*

4. The Bible never says that *sheol* was ever dug by a man or located on the earth, but this is said about a *grave.*

5. We never read in the Bible that man ever puts another man into *sheol,* but into a *grave.*

6. We read in the Bible that man touches a *grave,* but never read of him touching *sheol.*

So it is very evident that *sheol* and the *grave* are two different places.

In the New Testament there are three words in the Greek which are translated by the one word *hell*: *tartarus, hades,* and *gehenna.*

7

TARTARUS

The word *tartarus* occurs only once in the New Testament: "For is God spared not the angels that sinned, but cast them down to *hell,* and delivered them into chains of darkness, to be reserved unto judgment:" (II Peter 2:4). The word "hell" here is a translation of the verb form *tartarus* and it refers to a pit of darkness which serves as a prison house for certain angels who rebelled against God. They are further described in Jude 6: "And the angels which kept not their first estate, but left their own habitation, he hath reserved in everlasting chains under darkness unto the judgment of the great day" (Jude 6). These fallen angels are reserved under darkness awaiting their judgment which will take place when their leader, the devil, will be judged (Revelation 20:10), and they and the devil will be cast "into everlasting fire, prepared for the devil and his angels" (Matthew 25:41).

HADES

It is very definite that the two words *sheol* and *hades* are identical in meaning. The Septuagint is a Greek translation of the Old Testament which appeared 200 years before Christ. The translators were acquainted with both Hebrew and Greek and whenever they wanted to bring the Hebrew word *sheol* into Greek, they used the word *hades*. Of the sixty-five times the word *sheol* appears in the Old Testament, it was rendered into Greek by the word *hades* sixty-one times, twice by the word *death*, and twice it was omitted.

In Psalm 16:10 the Bible says: "For thou wilt not leave my soul in hell [Hebrew, *sheol*]; neither wilt thou suffer thine Holy One to see corruption." This verse speaks prophetically of Christ. This same verse is quoted in the New Testament in Acts 2:27: "Because thou wilt not leave my soul in hell [*hades*], neither wilt thou suffer thine Holy One to see corruption." (In Acts 2:31 we are told that this refers to the resurrection of Christ.)

Jesus' body went to the tomb, but His soul and spirit went into *hades* (*sheol*) when He died, and according to Matthew 12:40 He was there three days and three nights: "so shall the Son of man be three days and three nights in the heart of the earth." *Hades* and *sheol* were in "the heart of the earth" at that time. All of the people of the Old Testament who died went to *hades* or *sheol.*

In Luke 16:19-31 Jesus tells the story of two men who died, the rich man and Lazarus. Both of them went to *hades*, which at that time was divided into two compartments, one a place of torment (vv. 23, 24, 28), and one a place of comfort (v. 25). There was a "great gulf fixed" between the two compartments (v. 26), and although they could see each other, the people in each section could not pass from one section to the other.

The section of *hades* into which the righteous dead went was called "Abraham's bosom" (Luke 16:22) and "Paradise." Jesus told the repentant dying thief, "Today shalt thou be with me in paradise" (Luke 23:43), indicating that at death He went to "Paradise," and so did the thief who was saved. At that time "Paradise" was in the heart of the earth (Matthew 12:40), but when Jesus Christ rose from the dead He opened the "Paradise" section of *hades* and took the Old Testament saints into Heaven. We read about this in Ephesians 4:8-10: "Wherefore he saith, When he ascended up on high, he led captivity captive, and gave gifts unto men. (Now that he ascended, what is it but that he also descended first into the lower parts of the earth? He that descended is the same also that ascended up far above all heavens, that he might fill all things.)" Notice that it is said that "he descended first into the lower parts of the earth" (*hades* or *sheol*) (v. 9), and then He "ascended up on high" and "led captivity captive" (v. 8). The marginal reading is "He led a multitude of captives," and this speaks of the multitude of Old Testament saints who had been in the part of *hades* called "Abraham's bosom" or "Paradise" being led out by Jesus Christ at His ascension into Heaven.

9

"Paradise" is no longer in the heart of the earth but is now in the third heaven. Paul speaks of this in II Corinthians 12:2-4: "I knew a man in Christ above fourteen years ago, (whether in the body, I cannot tell; or whether out of the body, I cannot tell: God knoweth;) such an one caught up to the third heaven. And I knew such a man, (whether in the body, or out of the body, I cannot tell: God knoweth;) How that he was caught up into paradise, and heard unspeakable words, which it is not lawful for a man to utter." Paul says that he knew a man in Christ (himself) who was caught up to the third heaven in verse 2. (The first heaven is the region of the clouds, the second heaven the region of the planets, but the third heaven is the residence of God.) Then in verse 4 he said that he was "caught up into paradise."

Before Christ's resurrection and ascension, *hades* or *sheol* is always represented as being below and all the dead descended into it. After Christ's resurrection and ascension the spirits and souls of the saved people are spoken of as going up. Paul speaks of being "caught up to the third heaven" (II Corinthians 12:2) and being "caught up into paradise" (II Corinthians 12:4). Christ at His ascension went up to Heaven and the saints of the New Testament go to be with Him when they die. Paul said, "We are confident, I say, and willing rather to be absent from the body, and to be present with the Lord" (II Corinthians 5:8), and "For I am in a strait betwixt two, having a desire to depart, and to be with Christ; which is far better" (Philippians 1:23). To be absent from the body for a Christian means to be present with the Lord.

Jesus declared in Matthew 16:18: "I will build my church; and the gates of hell (*hades*) shall not prevail against it." When He led the Old Testament saints out, He locked the door and He holds the keys of hell (*hades*) and of death (Revelation 1:18). That compartment of *hades* will never be opened again to admit the soul of a saved person.

The reason the saints of the Old Testament went to

sheol-hades was because their sins were not yet taken away. Hebrews 10:4 says: "For it is not possible that the blood of bulls and goats should take away sins." God pardoned and passed by the sins of the saints of the Old Testament on the basis of the promise of the coming Redeemer. On the promissory note of Jesus that He would in the fulness of time pay the full debt for sin, God accepted the believer in the Old Testament. But when John the Baptist saw Jesus he exclaimed, "Behold the Lamb of God, which taketh away the sin of the world" (John 1:29). Also in Hebrews 9:26 God's Word says, "now once in the end of the world (completion of the ages) hath he [Christ] appeared to put away sin by the sacrifice of himself." Therefore when the sins of the Old Testament saints were put away or taken away by the sacrifice of Christ on the cross they could enter into the very presence of God.

No change occurred in the lost division of *hades* when Christ arose from the dead. The unsaved of all ages are still there, and all the spirits and souls of the people who die unsaved in the future will also go there.

In the New Testament *hades* occurs ten times. It is used by three writers of the New Testament: Matthew, Luke, and John. The word is found twice in Matthew (11:23; 16:18); twice in Luke (10:15; 16:23); twice in Acts (2:27,31); and four times in Revelation (1:18; 6:8; 20:13-14). The most detailed information about *hades* is found in Luke 16:19-31.

In this passage is the true story of two men who lived and died. Some people call this a parable, but it is not a parable. The Bible does not call it a parable. No names are used in parables, but in this story the names of Abraham and Lazarus are given. This is a true account of what happens after death. It is made clear here that the souls of men are conscious after death, that the wicked are in torment and the saved are comforted.

The rich man in *hades* could see: "And in hell (*hades*) he lift up his eyes . . . and seeth Abraham afar off and

Lazarus in his bosom" (v. 23).

He could speak: "And he cried and said . . ." (v. 24).

He wanted mercy: "Father Abraham, have mercy on me. . . ." (v. 24).

He wanted water: "send Lazarus, that he may dip the tip of his finger in water and cool my tongue. . . ." (v. 24).

He was tormented: "he lift up his eyes, being in torments. . . ." (v. 23); "I am tormented in this flame" (v. 24); "thou art tormented" (v. 25); "this place of torment" (v. 28).

He could remember: "Son, remember. . . ." (v. 25). Fred Stroble molested, ravished and then murdered a little girl in California. When the judge asked Stroble if he had any message before he pronounced the sentence, he replied, "I wake up in the night hearing the little girl ask me why I was killing her." He repeated over and over these words, "If I could only erase from my memory that girl's face and voice." So the sins committed by wicked people will be remembered and will taunt and torment them forever. People will remember the preaching they have heard, the promises they broke, the warnings they refused, the invitations they spurned, the opportunities to be saved they have missed.

No one could come to him and he could not get out: "between us and you there is a great gulf fixed: so that they which would pass from hence to you cannot; neither can they pass to us, that would come from thence" (v. 26).

He prayed for someone to go warn his five brothers: "Then he said, I pray thee therefore, father, that thou wouldest send him to my father's house: For I have five brethren; that he may testify unto them, lest they also come into this place of torment" (vv. 27-28). His request was not granted. He was told that his brothers had "Moses and the prophets [the Old Testament Scriptures]; let them hear them" (v. 29).

He knew he was in *hades* because he had not repented: "Nay, father Abraham: but if one went unto them from the dead, they will repent" (v. 30). He realized that people are lost because they do not repent and he wanted his brothers to repent so they would not come to the place where he was. He was told that if people do not listen to the Word of God and obey it, they wouldn't be persuaded "though one rose from the dead" (v. 31). Jesus warned, "I tell you, Nay: but, except ye repent, ye shall all likewise perish" (Luke 13:3).

It is very obvious from Luke 16:19-31 that there is no such thing as "soul-sleep" taught in the Bible. The rich man had all his faculties and was extremely conscious of the reality of the torment. This passage makes it clear also that there is absolutely no "second chance" after death to be saved. It refutes the false teaching of the annihilation of the soul, purgatory, soul-sleeping, and a second chance.

Hades is only a temporary abode for the unsaved. The eternal place of torment is not where the rich man went. Revelation 20:11-15 tells of the final judgment of the unsaved dead. Jesus, Who has the keys "of hell [*hades*] and of death" [the "grave"] (Revelation 1:18), will one day, at the close of the millennium, use these keys and will bring the bodies of the unsaved from their *graves* and the spirits and souls from *hades* and we read: "Death and hell [*hades*] delivered up the dead which were in them: and they were judged every man according to their works. And death and hell [*hades*] were cast into the lake of fire. This is the second death. And whosoever was not found written in the book of life was cast into the lake of fire" (Revelation 20:13-15).

Dr. M. R. DeHann, in his booklet *Heaven or Hell*, sums up so well what I have been saying that I quote him here:

Before the Cross of Calvary, . . . all of the dead who died from Adam on through the Old Testament dispensation went neither to heaven nor to hell. Their bodies were committed to the ground, buried in the graves or sepulchers, and their souls went into the place called hades. In the Old Testament it was called Sheol and this was divided into two compartments. The saved and redeemed

13

were put in a place of safety and comfort and joy, and expectation of their deliverance at the completion of the sacrificial work of the Lord Jesus Christ. Therefore David could say, "My flesh also shall rest in hope. For thou wilt not leave my soul in Sheol neither wilt thou suffer thine Holy One to see corruption." On the other hand, the lost were kept on the opposite side of sheol, separated from the redeemed by the great gulf, or the pit. In this place we find a description of what the eternal state of the lost will be. Remorse, and sorrow and suffering and torment and memory and utter hopelessness, because there is no escape once a man has died and his soul has gone into sheol.

Please notice carefully, therefore, that before the Cross, saints did not go to heaven, and sinners did not go to hell. Then when the Lord Jesus Christ came and hung upon the Cross of Calvary and paid the penalty for sin, one of His first acts after He had died was to go into the place called sheol-hades and there preached deliverance unto the saints who had been kept there because the penalty had not yet been fully paid, and triumphantly delivered them from sheol, and at His ascension at the first day of His resurrection He presented them in heaven, so that today all the Old Testament saints are in heaven, while their bodies still sleep in the grave, but every saint who dies today, does not go into sheol, but goes directly into the presence of Almighty God. The lost, however, in sheol, remain where they are until the judgment of the Great White Throne, and then, according to Revelation 20, the graves shall give up their bodies and sheol (hades) shall give up their souls, and they together will finally be cast into the Lake of Fire which is another description of the word hell, used in the New Testament.

GEHENNA

I come now to the last of the three words translated by the English word "Hell": *gehenna*. This is the final Hell to which every lost soul will be consigned for all eternity. This word is found twelve times in the New Testament: Matthew 5:22,29,30; 10:28; 18:9; 23:15,33; Mark 9:43,45,47; Luke 12:5; James 3:6. It is interesting to note that of the twelve times that this word is found in the

New Testament, Jesus used it eleven times.

It will be helpful here to give a chart showing every occurrence in the New Testament where the word "Hell" is mentioned:

TARTARUS — one time.	GEHENNA — twelve times.
II Peter 2:4	Matthew 5:22
HADES — ten times.	Matthew 5:29
	Matthew 5:30
Matthew 11:23	Matthew 10:28
Matthew 16:18	Matthew 18:9
Luke 10:15	Matthew 23:15
Luke 16:23	Matthew 23:33
Acts 2:37	Mark 9:43
Acts 2:31	Mark 9:45
Revelation 1:18	Mark 9:47
Revelation 6:8	Luke 12:5
Revelation 20:13	James 3:6
Revelation 20:14	

Gehenna, the lake of fire, and the second death are synonomous. Five times in the New Testament we read of the lake of fire: Revelation 19:20; Revelation 20:10; Revelation 20:14; Revelation 20:15; Revelation 21:8. The word *gehenna* comes from two Hebrew words "ge-hinnom" which mean "valley of Hinnom." Originally this valley was the property of a man by the name of Hinnom (II Kings 23:10). It is south of Jerusalem. In this valley there was a high place called "Tophet" (Isaiah 30:33; Jeremiah 7:31-32; 19:6,11,14) and some of the people of Israel offered their children as human sacrifices to the god Molech (Jeremiah 32:35). The sacrifices were bound and placed on the huge hands of the idol, whose arms formed a slide down into its interior which was a roaring furnace. Associated with this practice were rituals involving sexual perversions and the worship of the "hosts of heaven." God had commanded them: "And thou shalt not let any of thy seed [children] pass through the fire to Molech . . ." (Leviticus 18:21).

15

When Josiah the king destroyed the groves and high places of idolatry, the valley of Hinnom was turned into a city garbage and rubbish heap for burning the rubbish, as well as the bodies of dead animals and unburied criminals. To consume all of this, a fire burned continuously. Some of the garbage and decaying matter would lodge on the rocks of the wall and breed worms. Jesus used this known place with its burning fire and gnawing worms to teach truths about the unknown place—the final lake of fire. Hell is God's rubbish heap outside the New Jerusalem—where all that is unfit for the heavenly community will be discarded. Dr. A. C. Dixon commented: "Those who refuse life in God become 'refuse' in character sooner or later, and in the nature of things must be removed to a place apart." Six of the twelve references to *gehenna* mention "fire" as one of its characteristics: Matthew 5:22; 18:9; Mark 9:43,45,47; James 3:6.

No one is in this final place of punishment yet. The first occupants of this awful place will be the beast and the false prophet as described in Revelation 19:20: "And the beast was taken, and with him the false prophet that wrought miracles before him, with which he deceived them that had received the mark of the beast, and them that worshipped his image. These both were cast alive into a lake of fire burning with brimstone." This will occur at the conclusion of the tribulation period when Jesus returns to this earth to set up His millennial reign. These two men, called the beast and the false prophet, will be the political and religious leaders during the tribulation period, and will be cast alive into the lake of fire. As far as the Scriptures reveal, these two individuals will be the only two occupants of the lake of fire during the millennium. The rest of the wicked dead remain in *hades* throughout the thousand years (Revelation 20:5), and the devil will be in the bottomless pit during that time (Revelation 20:1-3).

The next individual who will be cast into the final Hell

16

will be the devil. After he is released at the close of the millennium, he goes out to deceive the nations, gathers a large army to follow him in his revolt against God, and then we read, "And the devil that deceived them was cast into the lake of fire and brimstone, where the beast and false prophet are, and shall be tormented day and night forever and ever" (Revelation 20:7-10). According to the words of Jesus in Matthew 25:41, everlasting fire was "prepared for the devil and his angels," and we conclude that when the devil is cast into the lake of fire, his angels (the fallen ones) will also be cast into the lake of fire. These fallen angels are the ones who followed Lucifer in his rebellion against God (Isaiah 14:12-15). Revelation 12:3-4 speaks of the dragon (another name for the devil or Satan) whose "tail drew the third part of the stars of heaven, and did cast them to the earth." A note in the Pilgrim Bible at verse four reads: "These are the Angels who followed Satan in his rebellion against God." Second Peter 2:4 says that "God spared not the angels that sinned, but cast them down to hell (*tartaros*) and delivered them into chains of darkness, to be reserved unto judgment," and Jude 6 speaks of "the angels which kept not their first estate, but left their own habitation, he hath reserved in everlasting chains under darkness until the judgment of the great day."

After the devil and his angels are cast into the final Hell, there will be the judgment of the Great White Throne spoken of in Revelation 20:11-15, and then all the wicked dead who have been resurrected and judged will be "cast into the lake of fire." Notice that death and hell (*hades*) will be cast into the lake of fire (Revelation 20:14). "Death" here refers to the grave which had received the body and "hell" refers to *hades* which had received the soul. Both body and soul will be cast into the lake of fire.

The purpose of this judgment at the Great White Throne is to see that absolute justice is given to every unsaved individual. Abraham asked the question: "Shall not the Judge of all the earth do right?" (Genesis 18:25). The answer, of course, is that He *will* do right and unsaved people will be "judged every man according to their works" (Revelation 20:13). The Bible says it will be more tolerable for some than for others. "Woe unto thee, Chorazin! woe unto thee, Bethsaida! for if the mighty works, which were done in you, had been done in Tyre and Sidon, they would have repented long ago in sackcloth and ashes. But I say unto you, It shall be more tolerable for Tyre and Sidon at the day of judgment, than for you. And thou, Capernaum, which are exalted unto heaven, shalt be brought down to hell: for if the mighty works, which have been done in thee, had been done in Sodom, it would have remained until this day. But I say unto you, That it shall be more tolerable for the land of Sodom in the day of judgment, than for thee." (Matthew 11:21-24). Christ spoke of the scribes and said of them, "the same shall receive greater damnation" (Luke 20:47). The difference in degrees will not be in the length of punishment, but in the severity of punishment. Throughout all eternity everyone will receive exactly what he deserves.

Jesus Christ said that the everlasting fire was "prepared for the devil and his angels" (Matthew 25:41). This everlasting fire was never meant for mankind. If a person goes there it will be because he chooses to do so by refusing God's gracious offer of eternal life. Jesus makes this plain in John 5:40: "And ye will not come to me, that ye might have life." He promises: "All that the Father giveth me shall come to me; and him that cometh to me I will in no wise cast out" (John 6:37). Nobody will ever be able to blame God for sending them to Hell. He is "not willing that any should perish, but that all should come to repentance" (II Peter 3:9).

Because of the widespread denial of Hell which is so prevalent today, I want to show what the Old Testament says about it; what Christ said about it; what the New Testament writers said about it; and then give some indirect references to it.

WHAT THE OLD TESTAMENT SAYS ABOUT HELL AND THE ETERNAL PUNISHMENT OF THE WICKED

"Even as I have seen, they that plow iniquity, and sow wickedness, reap the same. By the blast of God they perish, and by the breath of his nostrils are they consumed" (Job 4:8,9).

"But the eyes of the wicked shall fail, and they shall not escape, and their hope shall be as the giving up of the ghost" (Job 11:20).

"Yea, the light of the wicked shall be put out, and the spark of his fire shall not shine. The light shall be dark in his tabernacle, and his candle shall be put out with him. His remembrance shall perish from the earth, and he shall have no name in the street. He shall be driven from light into darkness, and chased out of the world" (Job 18:5,6,17,18).

"Surely such are the dwellings of the wicked, and this is the place of him that knoweth not God" (Job 18:21).

"For ye say, Where is the house of the prince? and where are the dwelling places of the wicked? Have ye not asked them that go by the way? and do ye not know their tokens, That the wicked is reserved to the day of destruction? they shall be brought forth to the day of wrath (Job 21:28-30).

"Is not destruction to the wicked? and a strange punishment to the workers of iniquity?" (Job 31:3).

"The ungodly are not so: but are like the chaff which the wind driveth away. Therefore the ungodly shall not stand in the judgment, nor sinners in the congregation of the righteous. For the LORD knoweth the way of the righteous: but the way of the ungodly shall perish" (Psalm 1:4-6).

"God judgeth the righteous and God is angry with the wicked every day. If he turn not, he will whet his sword; he hath bent his bow, and made it ready. He hath also prepared for him the instruments of death; he ordaineth his arrows against the persecutors" (Psalm 7:11-13).

"The wicked shall be turned into hell, and all the nations that forget God" (psalm 9:17).

"Upon the wicked he shall rain snares, fire and brimstone, and an horrible tempest: this shall be the portion of their cup." (Psalm 11:6).

"Thou shalt make them as a fiery oven in the time of thine anger: the LORD shall swallow them up in his wrath, and the fire shall devour them" (Psalm 21:9).

"But the wicked shall perish, and the enemies of the LORD shall be as the fat of lambs: they shall consume; into smoke shall they consume away" (Psalm 37:20).

"God shall likewise destroy thee forever, he shall take thee away, and pluck thee out of thy dwelling place, and root thee out of the land of the living. Selah" (Psalm 52:5).

"When I thought to know this, it was too painful for me; Until I went into the sanctuary of God; then understood I their end. Surely thou didst set them in slippery places: thou castedst them down into destruction. How are they brought into desolation, as in a moment! they are utterly consumed with terrors. As a dream when one awaketh; so, O Lord, when thou awakest, thou shalt despise their image. For, lo, they that are far from thee shall perish: thou hast destroyed all them that go a whoring from thee" (Psalm 73:16-20,27).

"When the wicked spring as the grass, and when all the workers of iniquity do flourish; it is that they shall be destroyed for ever" (Psalm 92:7).

"Salvation is far from the wicked: for they seek not thy statutes" (Psalm 119:115).

"The LORD preserveth all them that love him: but all the wicked will he destroy" (Psalm 145:20).

"But the wicked shall be cut off from the earth, and the transgressors shall be rooted out of it" (Proverbs 2:22).

"Her feet go down to death; her steps take hold on hell" (Proverbs 5:5).

"But he knoweth not that the dead are there; and that her guests are in the depths of hell" (Proverbs 9:18).

"The hope of the righteous shall be gladness: but the expection of the wicked shall perish" (Proverbs 10:28). "When a wicked man dieth, his expectation shall perish: and the hope of unjust men perisheth" (Proverbs 11:7).

"Though hand join in hand, the wicked shall not be unpunished: but the seed of the righteous shall be delivered" (Proverbs 11:21).

"The wicked is driven away in his wickedness: but the righteous hath hope in his death" (Proverbs 14:32).

"The way of life is above to the wise, that he may depart from hell beneath" (Proverbs 15:24).

"Everyone that is proud in heart is an abomination to the LORD: though hand join in hand, he shall not be unpunished" (Proverbs 16:5).

"Withhold not correction from the child: for if thou beatest him with the rod, he shall not die. Thou shalt beat him with the rod, and shalt deliver his soul from hell" (Proverbs 23:13,14).

"Woe unto the wicked! it shall be ill with him: for the reward of his hands shall be given him" (Isaiah 3:11).

"For Tophet is ordained of old; yea, for the king it is prepared; he hath made it deep and large: the pile thereof is fire and much wood; the breath of the LORD, like a stream of brimstone, doth kindle it" (Isaiah 30:33).

"The sinners in Zion are afraid; fearfulness hath surprised the hypocrites. Who among us shall dwell with the devouring fire? who among us shall dwell with everlasting burnings?" (Isaiah 33:14)

"And they shall go forth, and look upon the carcases of the men that have transgressed against me: for their worm shall not die, neither shall their fire be quenched; and they shall be an abhorring unto all flesh" (Isaiah 66:24).

"Now will I shortly pour out my fury upon thee, and accomplish mine anger upon thee: and I will judge thee according to thy ways, and will recompense thee for all thine abominations" (Ezekiel 7:8).

"And many of them that sleep in the dust of the earth shall awake, some to everlasting life, and some to shame and everlasting contempt" (Daniel 12:2).

"God is jealous, and the LORD revengeth; the LORD revengeth, and is furious; the LORD will take vengeance on his adversaries, and he reserveth wrath for his enemies. The LORD is slow to anger, and great in power, and will not at all acquit the wicked: the LORD hath his way in the whirlwind and in the storm, and the clouds are the dust of his feet" (Nahum 1:2,3).

Josephus, who was born four years after the ascension of Christ, whose learning and knowledge is not questioned, described with considerable care the religious belief of the Jews. He classified the Jews into three sects: Sadducees, Essenes, and Pharisees. Of the Sadducees he said, "They also take away the belief of the immortal duration of the soul, and the punishments and rewards in Hades." He said of the Essenes that they "allot to bad souls a dark and tempestuous den, full of never-ceasing punishments," and he said the Pharisees taught "the souls of bad men are subject to eternal punishment." (*The Works of Josephus*, "Wars of the Jews," Book II, Chapter 8).

According to the testimony of Josephus the vast majority of the Jewish nation, when Christ came into the world, were firm believers in the future everlasting punishment of the wicked.

WHAT CHRIST SAID ABOUT HELL AND THE ETERNAL PUNISHMENT OF THE WICKED

Some has said that Jesus was the greatest "Hell-fire Preacher" Who ever lived. He spoke more about Hell than He did about Heaven.

Even Theodore Parker, who did not believe in the everlasting punishment of the wicked, said, "To me it is quite clear that Jesus taught the doctrine of eternal damnation, if the evangelists — the first three, I mean —

are to be treated as inspired. I can understand His language in no other way."

Renan, who also did not believe in the everlasting punishment of the wicked, when he described the faith and teaching of Jesus, said, "The others [the wicked] will go into *Gehenna*. Gehenna was the valley west of Jerusalem. At various periods the worship of fire had been practiced in it, and the place had become a sort of *cloaca* [a receptacle of all manner of filth]. Gehenna is, therefore, in the mind of Jesus, a dismal valley, foul and full of fire. Those excluded from the kingdom will be burned and gnawed by worms, in company with Satan and his rebel angels. There, then, shall be weeping and gnashing of teeth . . . This new order of things will be eternal. Paradise and Gehenna shall have no end. . . .

"That all this was understood literally by the disciples and the Master Himself, at certain moments, stands forth absolutely evidenced in the writings of the time." (*Life of Jesus*, p. 243).

Thomas Paine and other infidels have made similar concessions, and deny the New Testament because it does teach the doctrine of everlasting punishment.

I have looked up the references in the four Gospels which give us what Jesus Christ said about Hell and everlasting punishment, and I give them here as they appear in these books. Some of these references are direct, others are indirect, but they all speak of the future punishment of the wicked.

"For I say unto you, That except your righteousness shall exceed the righteousness of the scribes and Pharisees, ye shall in no case enter into the kingdom of heaven. But I say unto you, That whosoever is angry with his brother without a cause shall be in danger of the judgment: and whosoever shall say to his brother, Raca, shall be in danger of the council: but whosoever shall say, Thou fool, shall be in danger of hell fire. And if thy right eye offend the, pluck it out, and cast it from thee: for it is profitable for thee that one of thy members should perish, and not that thy whole body should be cast into hell. And if thy right hand offend thee, cut it off, and cast it from thee: for it is profitable for thee that one of thy members should perish, and not that thy whole body should be cast into hell" (Matthew 5:20,22,29,30).

"Enter ye in at the strait gate: for wide is the gate, and broad is the way, that leadeth to destruction, and many there be which go in thereat: Not every one that saith unto me, Lord, Lord, shall enter into the kingdom of heaven; but he that doeth the will of my Father which is in heaven. Many will say to me in that day, Lord, Lord, have we not prophesied in thy name: and in thy name have cast out devils? and in thy name done many wonderful works? And then will I profess unto them, I never knew you: depart from me, ye that work iniquity. And every one that heareth these sayings of mine, and doeth them not, shall be likened unto a foolish man, which built his house upon the sand: And the rain descended, and the floods came, and the winds blew, and beat upon that house; and it fell: and great was the fall of it" (Matthew 7:13,21-23,26,27).

"And I say unto you, That many shall come from the east and west, and shall sit down with Abraham, and Isaac, and Jacob, in the kingdom of heaven. But the children of the kingdom shall be cast out into outer darkness: there shall be weeping and gnashing of teeth" (Matthew 8:11,12).

"And fear not them which kill the body, but are not able to kill the soul: but rather fear him which is able to destroy both soul and body in hell. But whosoever shall deny me before men, him will I also deny before my Father which is in heaven:" (Matthew 10:28,33).

"And thou, Capernaum, which are exalted unto heaven, shalt be brought down to hell: for if the mighty works, which have been done in thee, had been done in Sodom, it would have remained until this day. But I say unto you, That it shall be more tolerable for the land of Sodom in the day of judgment, than for thee" (Matthew 11:23,24).

"Wherefore I say unto you, All manner of sin and blasphemy shall be forgiven unto men: but the blasphemy against the Holy Ghost shall not be forgiven unto men. And whosoever speaketh a word against the Son of man, it shall be forgiven him: but whosoever speaketh against the Holy Ghost, it shall not be forgiven him, neither in this world, neither in the world to come" (Matthew 12:31,32).

"Let both grow together until the harvest: and in the time of harvest I will say to the reapers, Gather ye together first the tares, and bind them in bundles to burn them: but gather the wheat into my barn. As therefore the tares are gathered and burned in the fire; so shall it be in the end of this world. The Son of man shall send forth his angels, and they shall gather out of his kingdom all things that offend, and them which do iniquity; And shall cast them into a furnace of fire: there shall be wailing and gnashing of teeth. And shall cast them into the furnace of fire: there shall be wailing and gnashing of teeth" (Matthew 13:30,40-42,50).

"And said, Verily I say unto you, Except ye be converted, and become as little children, ye shall not enter into the kingdom of heaven. Wherefore if thy hand or thy foot offend thee, cut them off, and cast them from thee: it is better for thee to enter into life halt or maimed, rather than having two hands or two feet to be cast into everlasting fire. And if thine eye offend thee, pluck it out, and cast it from thee: it is better for thee to enter into life with one eye, rather than having two eyes to be cast into hell fire" (Matthew 18:3,8,9).

"They say unto him, He will miserably destroy those wicked men, and will let out his vineyard unto other husbandmen, which shall render him the fruits in their seasons. And whosoever shall fall on this stone shall be broken: but on whomsoever it shall fall, it will grind him to powder" (Matthew 21:41,44).

"And he saith unto him, Friend, how camest thou in hither not having a wedding garment? And he was speechless. Then said the king to the servants, Bind him hand and foot, and take him away, and cast him into outer darkness; there shall be weeping and gnashing of teeth" (Matthew 22:12,13).

"Ye serpents, ye generation of vipers, how can ye escape the damnation of hell?" (Matthew 23:33).

"Then shall he say also unto them on the left hand, Depart from me, ye cursed, into everlasting fire, prepared for the devil and his angels: And these shall go away into everlasting punishment: but the righteous into life eternal" (Matthew 25:41,46).

"The Son of man goeth as it is written of him: but woe unto that man by whom the Son of man is betrayed! it had been good for that man if he had not been born" (Matthew 26:24).

"Verily I say unto you, All sins shall be forgiven unto the sons of men, and blasphemies wherewith soever they shall blaspheme: But he that shall blaspheme against the Holy Ghost hath never forgiveness, but is in danger of eternal damnation" (Mark 3:28,29).

"And if thy hand offend thee, cut it off: it is better for thee to enter into life maimed, than having two hands to go into hell, into the fire that never shall be quenched: Where their worm dieth not, and the fire is not quenched. And if thy foot offend thee, cut it off: it is better for thee to enter halt into life, than having two feet to be cast into hell, into the fire that never shall be quenched: Where their worm dieth not, and the fire is not quenched. And if thine eye offend thee, pluck it out: it is better for thee to enter into the kingdom of God with one eye, than having two eyes to be cast into hell fire: Where their worm dieth not, and the fire is not quenched" (Mark 9:43-48).

"He that believeth and is baptized shall be saved; but he that believeth not shall be damned" (Mark 16:16).

"Then said he to the multitude that came forth to be baptized of him, O generation of vipers, who hath warned you to flee from the wrath to come? Whose fan is in his hand, and he will throughly purge his floor, and will gather the wheat into his garner; but the chaff he will burn with fire unquenchable" (Luke 3:7,17).

"Woe unto thee, Chorazin! woe unto thee, Bethsaida! for if the mighty works had been done in Tyre and Sidon, which have been done in you, they had a great while ago repented, sitting in sackcloth and ashes. But it shall be more tolerable for Tyre and Sidon at the judgment, than for you. And thou, Capernaum, which art exalted to heaven, shalt be thrust down to hell" (Luke 10:13-15).

"But I will forewarn you whom ye shall fear: Fear him, which after he hath killed hath power to cast into hell; yea, I say unto you, Fear him" (Luke 12:5).

"I tell you, Nay: but, except ye repent, ye shall all likewise perish. I tell you, Nay: but, except ye repent, ye shall all likewise perish" (Luke 13:3,5).

"Strive to enter in at the strait gate: for many, I say unto you, will seek to enter in, and shall not be able. When once the master of the house is risen up, and hath shut to the door, and ye begin to stand without, and to knock at the door, saying, Lord, Lord, open unto us; and he shall answer and say unto you, I know you not whence ye are: Then shall ye begin to say, we have eaten and drunk in thy presence, and thou hast taught in our streets. But he shall say, I tell you, I know you not whence ye are; depart from me, all ye workers of iniquity. There shall be weeping and gnashing of teeth, when ye shall see Abraham, and Isaac, and Jacob, and all the prophets, in the kingdom of God, and your yourselves thrust out" (Luke 13:24-28).

"There was a certain rich man, which was clothed in purple and fine linen, and fared sumptuously every day: And there was a certain beggar named Lazarus, which was laid at his gate full of sores, And desiring to be fed with the crumbs which fell from the rich man's table: moreover the dogs came and licked his sores. And it came to pass, that the begger died, and was carried by the angels into Abraham's bosom: the rich man also died, and was buried; And in hell he lift up his eyes, being in torments, and seeth Abraham afar off, and Lazarus in his bosom. And he cried and said, Father Abraham, have mercy on me, and send Lazarus, that he may dip the tip of his finger in water, and cool my tongue; for I am tormented in this flame. But Abraham said, Son, remember that thou in thy lifetime receivedst thy good things, and likewise Lazarus evil things: but now he is comforted, and thou are tormented. And beside all this, between us and you there is a great gulf fixed: so that they which would pass from hence to you cannot; neither can they pass to us, that would come from thence. Then he said, I pray thee therefore, father, that thou wouldest send him to my father's house: for I have five brethren; that he may testify unto them, lest they also come into this place of torment. Abraham saith unto him, They have Moses and the prophets; let them hear them. And he said, Nay, father Abraham: but if one went unto them from the dead, they will repent. And he said unto him, If they hear not Moses and the prophets, neither will they be persuaded, though one rose from the dead" (Luke 16:19-31).

"That whosoever believeth in Him should not perish, but have eternal life. For God so loved the world, that he gave his only begotten Son, that whosoever believeth in him should not perish, but have everlasting life" (John 3:15,16).

"He that believeth on him is not condemned: but he that believeth not is condemned already, because he hath not believed in the name of the only begotten Son of God. He that believeth on the Son hath everlasting life: and he that believeth not the Son shall not see life; but the wrath of God abideth on him" (John 3:18,36).

"Marvel not at this: for the hour is coming, in the which all that are in the graves shall hear his voice, And shall come forth; they that have done good, unto the resurrection of life: and they that have done evil, unto the resurrection of damnation" (John 5:28,29).

"Ye shall seek me, and shall not find me: and where I am, thither ye cannot come" (John 7:34).

"Then said Jesus again unto them, I go my way, and ye shall seek me, and shall die in your sins: whither I go, ye cannot come. I said therefore unto you, that ye shall die in your sins: for if ye believe not that I am he, ye shall die in your sins" (John 8:21,24).

"While I was with them in the world, I kept them in thy name: those that thou gavest me I have kept, and none of them is lost, but the son of perdition; that the scripture might be fulfilled" (John 17:12).

Every time the word *hell* is used in the first three Gospels, Jesus Christ used it. Matthew records it nine times, Mark three times, and Luke three times.

There are many people who think of Christ as "Gentle Jesus, meek and mild." They refer to His Sermon on the Mount as the kind of preaching they like. I remind them that three times in this one sermon Jesus spoke of Hell: Matthew 5:22,29,30.

If we believe the Bible to be true, we must believe that Jesus taught very definitely that there is a Hell. Leslie H. Woodson remarks: "Evidence is sufficient for the belief that Jesus shared the idea of a fiery hell for the wicked" (*Hell and Salvation*, p. 20).

WHAT THE APOSTLES SAID ABOUT HELL AND THE ETERNAL PUNISHMENT OF THE WICKED

What Paul Said About Hell and Judgment

"Beware therefore, lest that come upon you, which is spoken of in the prophets; Behold, ye despisers, and wonder, and perish: for I work a work in your days, a work which ye shall in no wise believe, though a man declare it unto you. Then Paul and Barnabas waxed bold, and said, It was necessary that the word of God should first have been spoken to you: but seeing ye put it from you, and judge yourselves unworthy of everlasting life, lo, we turn to the Gentiles" (Acts 13:40,41,46).

"For the wrath of God is revealed from heaven against all ungodliness and unrighteousness of men, who hold the truth in unrighteousness" (Romans 1:18).

"But after thy hardness and impenitent heart treasurest up unto thyself wrath against the day of wrath and revelation of the righteous judgment of God; Who will render to every man according to his deeds: To them who by patient continuance in well doing seek for glory and honour and immortality, eternal life: But unto them that are contentious, and do not obey the truth, but obey unrighteousness, indignation and wrath, Tribulation and anguish, upon every soul of man that doeth evil, of the Jew first, and also of the Gentile" (Romans 2:5-9).

"For the wages of sin is death; but the gift of God is eternal life through Jesus Christ our Lord" (Romans 6:23).

"What if God, willing to shew his wrath, and to make his power known, endured with much longsuffering the vessels of wrath fitted to destruction" (Romans 9:22).

"Know ye not that the unrighteous shall not inherit the kingdom of God? Be not deceived: neither fornicators, nor idolaters, nor adulterers, nor effeminate, nor abusers of themselves with mankind, Nor thieves, nor covetous, nor drunkards, nor revilers, not extortioners, shall inherit the kingdom of God" (I Corinthians 6:9,10).

"But though we, or an angel from heaven, preach any other gospel unto you than that which we have preached unto you, let him be accursed. As we said before, so say I now again, If any man preach any other gospel unto you than that ye have received, let him be accursed" (Galatians 1:8,9).

"For as many as are of the works of the law are under the curse: for it is written, Cursed is every one that continueth not in all things which are written in the book of the law to do them" (Galatians 3:10).

"Now the works of the flesh are manifest, which are these; Adultery, fornication, uncleanness, lasciviousness, Idolatry, witchcraft, hatred, variance, emulations, wrath, strife, seditions, heresies, Envyings, murders, drunkenness, revellings, and such like: of the which I tell you before, as I have also told you in time past, that they which do such things shall not inherit the kingdom of God" (Galatians 5:19-21).

"For this ye know, that no whoremonger, nor unclean person, nor covetous man, who is an idolater, hath any inheritance in the kingdom of Christ and of God. Let no man deceive you with vain words: for because of these things cometh the wrath of God upon the children of disobedience" (Ephesians 5:5,6).

"Wherefore God also hath highly exalted him, and given him a name which is above every name; That at the name of Jesus every knee should bow, of things in heaven, and things in earth, and things under the earth; And that every tongue should confess that Jesus Christ is Lord, to the glory of God the Father" (Philippians 2:9-11).

"For many walk, of whom I have told you often, and now tell you even weeping, that they are the enemies of the cross of Christ: Whose end is destruction, whose God is their belly, and whose glory is in their shame, who mind earthly things" (Philippians 3:18,19).

"Mortify therefore your members which are upon the earth; fornication, uncleanness, inordinate affection, evil concupiscence, and covetousness, which is idolatry: For which things' sake the wrath of God cometh on the children of disobedience" (Colossians 3:5,6).

"But he that doeth wrong shall receive for the wrong which he hath done: and there is no respect of persons" (Colossians 3:25).

"And to you who are troubled rest with us, when the Lord Jesus shall be revealed from heaven with his mighty angels, In flaming fire taking vengeance on them that know not God, and that obey not the gospel of our Lord Jesus Christ: Who shall be punished with everlasting destruction from the presence of the Lord, and from the glory of his power" (II Thessalonians 1:7-9).

"And with all deceivableness of unrighteousness in them that perish; because they received not the love of the truth, that they might be saved. And for this cause God shall send them strong delusion, that they should believe a lie: That they all might be damned who believed not the truth, but had pleasure in unrighteousness" (II Thessalonians 2:10-12).

"Some men's sins are open beforehand, going before to judgment; and some men they follow after" (I Timothy 5:24).

"But they that will be rich fall into temptation and a snare, and into many foolish and hurtful lusts, which drown men in destruction and perdition" (I Timothy 6:9).

"And as it is appointed unto men once to die, but after this the judgment" (Hebrews 9:27).

What Peter Said About Hell and Judgment

"And it shall come to pass, that every soul, which will not hear that prophet, shall be destroyed from among the people" (Acts 3:23).

"For the time is come that judgment must begin at the house of God: and if it first begin at us, what shall the end be of them that obey not the gospel of God? And if the righteous scarcely be saved, where shall the ungodly and the sinner appear?" (I Peter 4:17,18).

"But there were false prophets also among the people, even as there shall be false teachers among you, who privily shall bring in damnable heresies, even denying the Lord that bought them, and bring upon themselves swift destruction. And many shall follow their pernicious ways; by reason of whom the way of truth shall be evil spoken of. And through covetousness shall they with feigned words make merchandise of you: whose judgment now of a long time lingereth not, and their damnation slumbereth not. For if God spared not the angels that sinned, but cast them down to hell, and delivered them into chains of darkness, to be reserved unto judgment; And spared not the old world, but saved Noah the eighth person, a preacher of righteousness, bringing in the flood upon the world of the ungodly; And turning the cities of Sodom and Gomorrha into ashes condemned them with an overthrow, making them an ensample unto those that after should live ungodly; And delivered just Lot, vexed with the filthy conversation of the wicked: (For that righteous man dwelling among them, in seeing and hearing, vexed his righteous soul from day to day with their unlawful deeds;) The Lord knoweth how to deliver the godly out of temptations, and to reserve the unjust unto the day of judgment to be punished: But these, as natural brute beasts, made to be taken and destroyed, speak evil of the things that they understand not; and shall utterly perish in their own corruption" (II Peter 2:1-9,12).

"But the heavens and the earth, which are now, by the same word are kept in store, reserved unto fire against the day of judgment and perdition of ungodly men. As also in all his epistles, speaking in them of these things; in which are some things hard to be understood, which they that are unlearned and unstable wrest, as they do also the other scriptures, unto their own destruction" (II Peter 3:7,16).

What James Said About Hell and Judgment

"Let him know, that he which converteth the sinner from the error of his way, shall save a soul from death, and shall hide a multitude of sins" (James 5:20).

What Jude Said About Hell and Judgment

"Even as Sodom and Gomorrha, and the cities about them in like manner, giving themselves over to fornication, and going after strange flesh, are set forth for an example, suffering the vengeance of eternal fire. Woe unto them! for they have gone in the way of Cain, and ran greedily after the error of Balaam for reward, and perished in the gainsaying of Core. These are spots in your feasts of charity, when they feast with you, feeding themselves without fear: clouds they are without water, carried about of winds; trees whose fruit withereth, without fruit, twice dead, plucked up by the roots; Raging waves of the sea, foaming out their own shame; wandering stars, to whom is reserved the blackness of darkness for ever" (Jude 7,11-13).

What John Said About Hell and Judgment

"Whosoever hateth his brother is a murderer: and ye know that no murderer hath eternal life abiding in him" (I John 3:15).

"He that hath the Son hath life; and he that hath not the Son of God hath not life" (I John 5:12).

"And all that dwell upon the earth shall worship him, whose names are not written in the book of life of the Lamb slain from the foundation of the world" (Revelation 13:8).

"And the third angel followed them, saying with a loud voice, If any man worship the beast and his image, and receive his mark in his forehead, or in his hand, The same shall drink of the wine of the wrath of God, which is poured out without mixture into the cup of his indignation; and he shall be tormented with fire and brimstone in the presence of the holy angels, and in the presence of the Lamb: And the smoke of their torment ascendeth up for ever and ever: and they have no rest day nor night, who worship the beast and his image, and whosoever receiveth the mark of his name" (Revelation 14:9-11).

"The beast that thou sawest was, and is not; and shall ascend out of the bottomless pit, and go into perdition: and they that dwell on the earth shall wonder, whose names were not written in the book of life from the foundation of the world, when they behold the beast that was, and is not, and yet is" (Revelation 17:8).

"And the beast was taken, and with him the false prophet that wrought miracles before him, with which he deceived them that had received the mark of the beast, and them that worshipped his image. These both were cast alive into a lake of fire burning with brimstone" (Revelation 19:20).

"And the devil that deceived them was cast into the

lake of fire and brimstone, where the beast and the false prophet are, and shall be tormented day and night for ever and ever. And I saw a great white throne, and him that sat on it, from whose face the earth and the heaven fled away; and there was found no place for them. And I saw the dead, small and great, stand before God; and the books were opened: and another book was opened, which is the book of life: and the dead were judged out of those things which were written in the books, according to their works. And the sea gave up the dead which were in it; and death and hell delivered up the dead which were in them: and they were judged every man according to their works. And death and hell were cast into the lake of fire. This is the second death. And whosoever was not found written in the book of life was cast into the lake of fire" (Revelation 20:10-15).

"But the fearful, and unbelieving, and the abominable, and murderers, and whoremongers, and sorcerers, and idolaters, and all liars, shall have their part in the lake which burneth with fire and brimstone: which is the second death. And there shall in no wise enter into it any thing that defileth, neither whatsoever worketh abomination, or maketh a lie: but they which are written in the Lamb's book of life" (Revelation 21:8,27).

"He that is unjust, let him be unjust still: and he which is filthy, let him be filthy still: and he that is righteous, let him be righteous still: and he that is holy, let him be holy still. For without are dogs, and sorcerers, and whoremongers, and murderers, and idolaters, and whosoever loveth and maketh a lie. And if any man shall take away from the words of the book of this prophecy, God shall take away his part out of the book of life, and out of the holy city, and from the things which are written in this book" (Revelation 22:11,15,19).

Merrill F. Unger, in his *Bible Dictionary*, states, "Of the fact of future punishment and of the eternal duration in some form the teachings of Christ and the apostles leave no room for doubt" (p. 901).

WHAT THE BIBLE SAYS AS IT DESCRIBES HELL AND EVERLASTING PUNISHMENT

Hell is described from A to Z in the Bible. Some of the descriptions are given here.

HELL FROM A TO Z

Hell will be a place of:

A — ABIDING WRATH

"He that believeth on the Son hath everlasting life: and he that believeth not the Son shall not see life; but the wrath of God abideth on him" (John 3:36). This verse says that the wrath of God abides on the sinner right now and if he dies unsaved God's wrath will abide on him forever. The Greek word for wrath is *orge* and is used twelve times in the book of Romans alone and always refers to God's wrath: "For the *wrath* of God is revealed from heaven against all ungodliness and unrighteousness of men, who hold the truth in unrighteousness" (Romans 1:18).

"But after thy hardness and impenitent heart treasurest up unto thyself *wrath* against the day of *wrath* and revelation of the righteous judgment of God; But unto them that are contentious, and do not obey the truth, but obey unrighteousness, indignation and *wrath*" (Romans 2:5,8).

"God is jealous, and the LORD revengeth; the LORD revengeth, and is furious; the LORD will take vengeance on his adversaries, and he reserveth *wrath* for his enemies" (Nahum 1:2).

William R. Newell comments on the wrath of God:

Let this awful word *Orge*, Wrath, settle into the conscience of every soul; for God hath spoken it!

And every Preacher, and every Prophet *of God* has warned of it: Enoch (Jude 14,15); Noah (II Pet. 2:5); Moses (Deut. 32:35); the Psalmists, the Prophets (for

36

example, Isaiah, — all of chapters 24 and 34); the Lord's forerunner, John the Baptist, with his 'Flee from the wrath to come;' the Apostles, — from Romans to Revelation; and the great Preachers and Evangelists of the Christian centuries, — the men who have won souls — the Reformers, the Puritans, the Wesleys, Whitfields, Edwardses, Finneys, Spurgeons, Moodys, — all have told of man's guilt and danger, of the coming judgment, and of the wrath of God upon the impenitent and unbelieving." (Romans Verse by Verse, p. 42).

In his famous sermon "Sinners in the Hands of An Angry God," Jonathan Edwards warned his hearers of the wrath of God:

There are the black clouds of God's wrath now hanging directly over your heads, full of the dreadful storm, and big with thunder; and were it not for the restraining hand of God it would immediately burst forth upon you. The sovereign pleasure of God, for the present, stays His rough wind. Otherwise it would come with fury, and your destruction would come like a whirlwind, and you would be like the chaff of the summer threshing floor.

The wrath of God is like great waters that are damned for the present. They increase more and more, and rise higher and higher, till an outlet is given. The longer the stream is stopped, the more rapid and mighty is its course, when once it is let loose . . .

The bow of God's wrath is bent, and the arrow made ready on the string, and justice bends the arrow at your heart and strains the bow, and it is nothing but the mere pleasure of God, and of an angry God, without any promise or obligation at all, that keeps the arrow one moment from being made drunk with your blood. . . .

Consider the fearful danger you are in! It is a great furnace of wrath, a wide and bottomless pit, full of the fire of wrath, that you are held over in the hand of that God whose wrath is provoked and incensed as much against you as against many of the damned in Hell. You hang by a slender thread, with the flames of divine wrath flashing about it, and ready every moment to singe it and burn it asunder. You have no interest in any Mediator, and nothing to lay hold of to save yourself, nothing to keep off the flames of wrath, nothing of your own, nothing that you have ever done, nothing that you can do, to induce God to spare you one moment.

And consider here more particularly whose wrath it is. It is the wrath of an infinite God. . . .

It is the fierceness of His wrath that you are exposed to. . . .

Thus we read of "the winepress of the fierceness and wrath of Almighty God" (Rev. 19:15). The words are exceedingly terrible, if only it had been said, "the wrath of God", the word would have implied that which is infinitely dreadful. But it is said, "the fierceness and wrath of God". The fury of God! The fierceness of Jehovah! Oh, how dreadful must that be!

It is everlasting wrath. It would be dreadful to suffer this fierceness and wrath of Almghty God one moment; but you must suffer it for all eternity. There will be no end to this exquisite, horrible misery. . . .

How dreadful is the state of those that are daily and hourly in danger of this great wrath and infinite misery! But this is the dismal case of every soul that has not been born again, however moral and strict, sober and religious, they may otherwise be. Oh, that you would consider it, whether you are young or old! . . .

Therefore, let every one that is out of Christ now awake and flee from the wrath to come. The wrath of Almighty God is now undoubtedly hanging over every unregenerate sinner. (*Great Sermons by Great Preachers*, pp. 30, 31, 33, 34, 35, 39, 40, 44).

Thank God, because Jesus Christ suffered the wrath of God against sin at Calvary, when we trust Him as our personal Lord and Saviour, we have God's gracious promise: "Much more then, being now justified by his blood, we shall be saved from *wrath* through him" (Romans 5:9).

B — BLACKNESS OF DARKNESS FOREVER

"Raging waves of the sea, foaming out their own shame; wandering stars, to whom is reserved *the blackness of darkness for ever*" (Jude 13).

God says in I Samuel 2:9: "the wicked shall be silent in *darkness*." They will be so stunned and dumbfounded with the condition in which they find themselves that they will be speechless. Psalm 49:19 says, "they shall never see light." Peter speaks concerning the wicked: "to whom the mist of *darkness* is reserved forever" (II Peter 2:17).

Think of a place without the sun, moon, stars; without an electric light, lamp light, candlelight, or lightning bug, but forever darkness. Think also of people being like "wandering stars," going round and round in space, totally alone, just wandering, forever and ever. This is the reservation for the wicked. It is bad enough to see people in this life drifting with no purpose, but for this to extend throughout all eternity is so awful the mind cannot dwell upon it very long.

Jesus spoke of those who "loved *darkness* rather than light, because their deeds were evil" (John 3:19), and since they hate the light and do not come to the light (John 3:20), they get *darkness* forever. Jesus also spoke of those who "shall be cast out into outer *darkness*: there shall be weeping and gnashing of teeth" (Matthew 8:12).

Job speaks of the wicked and says, "He shall be driven from light into *darkness*, and chased out of the world" (Job 18:18).

Robert L. Summer, in his well-written book, *Hell Is No Joke*, said: "I remember hearing the noted evangelist and university founder, Bob Jones, tell of a lady who trained her pet parrot to say 'Good night' and 'Good morning.' Each evening she would place a cloth covering over the parrot's cage and say, 'Good night, Polly,' and the parrot would respond, 'Good night.' In the morning as she lifted the cover off the cage she would say, 'Good morning, Polly,' and the parrot would say, 'Good morning.'

"One day the parrot escaped from his cage momentarily and before it was discovered he got into a fight with the family cat. That night when his mistress covered his cage and said, 'Good night, Polly,' he immediately responded with the usual, 'Good night.' However, when she lifted the cloth from the cage the following day and said, 'Good morning, Polly,' the parrot replied, 'Good night.'

Shocked at his mistake, she replied again, 'Good morning, Polly,' only to have him reply the second time, 'Good night.' Closer examination revealed the parrot's eyes had been scratched out the day before in the fight with the cat and Polly would never again know 'Good morning' — only 'Good night.'

"Hell is an eternal 'Good night' for every sinner who leaves this life without Christ. Never again will he have a 'Good morning' since the sun never rises in that land of anguish and despair. What a terrible thing it is to be lost!" (*Hell is no Joke*, pp. 18-19).

Though there is for the lost "the blackness of darkness forever," Jesus said, "I am the light of the world: he that followeth me shall not walk in darkness, but shall have the light of life" (John 8:12).

C — CRYING

At least five times in the New Testament Jesus speaks of people in outer darkness weeping and gnashing their teeth (Matthew 8:12; 22:13; 24:51; 25:30; Luke 13:28). It is said of the rich man in Hell "he cried" (Luke 16:24). John Bunyan has written an article concerning this crying entitled "A Sigh from Hell":

> He was laughing, jesting, jeering, drinking, mocking, swearing, cursing, prating, persecuting the godly in his prosperity, among his filthy companions. But now the case is otherwise, now he is in another frame, now his proud, stout, currish carriage is come down; "And he cried." The laughter of the ungodly will not last always, but will be sure to end in a cry: "The triumphing of the wicked is short." — Job 20:5.

> Consider, you must have a change either here or in Hell. If you be not new creatures, regenerate persons, and newborn babes, in this world, before you go hence, your note will be changed, your conditions will be changed; for if you come into Hell, you must cry. . . .

> O what an alteration will there be among the ungodly when they go out of this world! It may be a fortnight, or a month before their departure, they were light, stout, surly, drinking themselves drunk, slighting God's people,

40

mocking at goodness, and delighting in sin, following the world, seeking after riches, faring deliciously, keeping company with the wickedest; but now, they are dropped down into Hell, they cry.

Little while ago they were painting their faces, feeding their lusts, following their whores, robbing their neighbors, telling their lies, following plays and sports, to pass away the time; but now they are in Hell, they do cry.

It may be last year they heard some good sermon, were invited to receive Heaven, were told their sins should be pardoned if they closed in with Jesus; but, refusing His proffers, and slighting the grace that was once tendered, they are now in Hell, and do cry.

Before, they had so much time, they thought that they could not tell how to spend it, unless it were in hunting and whoring, in dancing, and playing, and spending whole hours, yea days, yea weeks, in the lusts of the flesh; but when they depart into another place, they begin to lift up their eyes in Hell, and consider their miserable and irrecoverable condition, they cry.

O what a condition wilt thou fall into, when thou dost depart this world; if thou depart unconverted, and not born again, thou hadst better have been smothered the first hour thou wast born; thou hadst better have been plucked one limb from another; thou hadst better have been made a dog, a toad, a serpent, nay, any other creature in the visible world, then to die unconverted; and this thou wilt find to be true, when in Hell thou dost lift up thine eyes, and dost cry.

Here then, you may see that it is not without good ground that these words are here spoken by our Lord, that when any of the ungodly depart into Hell, they will cry. Cry, who so?

(1) They will cry to think that they should be cut off from the land of the living, never more to have any footing therein.

(2) They will cry to think that the Gospel of Christ should be so often proffered them and yet they are not profited by it.

(3) They will cry to think that now, though they would never so willingly repent and be saved, yet they are past all recovery.

(4) They will cry to think that they should be so foolish

as to follow their pleasures, when others were following Christ (Luke 13:28).

(5) They will cry to think that they must be separated from God, Christ, and the kingdom of Heaven, and that forever.

(6) To think that their crying will do them no good.

(7) To think that, at the day of judgment, they must stand at the left hand of Christ, among an innumerable company of the damned ones.

(8) They will cry to think that Lazarus, whom they once slighted, must be of them that must sit down with Christ to judge, or together with Christ, to pass a sentence of condemnation on their souls forever and ever (I Cor. 6:2,3).

(9) Cry to think that when the judgment is over, and others are taken into the everlasting kingdom of glory, then they must depart back again into that dungeon of darkness from whence they came out, to appear before the terrible tribunal. There they shall be tormented so long as eternity lasts, without the least intermission or ease.

How sayest thou, O thou wanton, proud, swearing, lying, ungodly wretch, whether this is to be slighted and made a mock at? And again, tell me now, if it be not better to leave sin, and to close in with Christ Jesus, notwithstanding that reproach thou shalt meet with for so doing, than to live a little while in this world in pleasures and feeding thy lusts, in neglecting the welfare of thy soul, and refusing to be justified by Jesus; and in a moment to drop down to Hell and to cry?

O! consider, I say, consider betimes, and put not off the tenders of the grace of our Lord Jesus Christ, lest you lift up your eyes in Hell, and cry for anguish of spirit. (Tract, "A Sigh from Hell").

D — DAMNATION

"But he that shall blaspheme against the Holy Ghost hath never forgiveness, but is in danger of eternal *damnation*" (Mark 3:29). Jesus asked the question, "how can you escape the *damnation* of hell?" (Matthew 23:33).

"He that believeth and is baptized shall be saved; but he that believeth not shall be *damned*" (Mark 16:16).

"And shall come forth; they that have done good, unto

the resurrection of life; and they that have done evil, unto the resurrection of *damnation*" (John 5:29).

Paul spoke of those who refused the truth and were not saved and said of them: "That they all might be *damned* who believed not the truth, but had pleasure in unrighteousness" (II Thessalonians 2:12).

Here are the testimonies of people when they came to die, who realized they were damned:

TALLEYRAND PERIGORD: "I am suffering the pangs of the damned."

SIR THOMAS SCOTT: "Until this moment I believed that there was neither a God nor a hell. Now I know and feel there are both and I am doomed to perdition by the just judgment of the Almighty."

THOMAS PAINE: "I would give worlds, if I had them, if the 'Age of Reason' had never been published. O Lord, help me! Christ, help me! Stay with me! It is hell to be left alone!"

FRANCIS NEWPORT: "That there is a God, I know, because I continually feel the effects of His wrath; that there is a hell, I am equally certain, having received an earnest of my inheritance there already in my breast. I have despised my Maker and denied my Redeemer; I have joined myself to the atheist and profane, and continued this course under many convictions, till my iniquity was ripe for vengeance and the just judgment of God.

"How idle is it to bid the fire not burn when fuel is administered, and to command the seas to be smooth in the midst of a storm! Such is my case; and what are the comforts of my friends? Whither am I going? Damned and lost forever. God has become my enemy and there is none able to save me. Oh, the insufferable pangs of hell and damnation!"

VOLTAIRE: "I am abandoned by God and man! I shall go to hell! O Christ! O Jesus Christ!"

CHARLES IX, KING OF FRANCE: "What blood, what evil counsels have I followed! I am lost; I see it well!"

HOBBES: "I say again, if I had the whole world to dispose of, I would give it to live one day. I am about to take a leap in the dark!"

GIBBON: "All is now lost, finally, irrecoverably lost. All is dark and doubtful!"

QUEEN ELIZABETH: "All my possessions but for a moment of time!"

CHARTERES: "I would gladly give thirty thousand pounds to have it proved there is no hell."

MIRABEAU: "Give me more laudanum that I may not think of eternity."

SIR THOMAS SMITH: "It is lamentable that men consider not for what end they are born into the world till they are ready to go out of it."

CAESAR BORGIA: "I have provided, in the course of my life, for everything except death. Now, alas! I am to die, although entirely unprepared!"

JENNIE GORDON: "The fiends, they come; O save me! They drag me down! Lost! Lost! Lost! Bind me, ye chains of darkness! Oh! that I might cease to be, but still exist. The worm that never dies, the second death."

NAPOLEON BONAPARTE: "I died before my time, and my body will be given back to the earth to become food for worms. Such is the fate of him who has been called the great Napoleon. What an abyss lies between my deep misery and the eternal kingdom of Christ!"

E — EVERLASTING PUNISHMENT

"And these shall go away into everlasting punishment: but the righteous into life eternal" (Matthew 25:46).
I have made a detailed study of the word *Aionios*,

which means "eternal" or "everlasting" and in chapter 2 I show this word refers to punishment of the wicked as eternal or everlasting. William Elbert Munsey wrote of the everlasting punishment of the wicked:

"The eternal punishment of the wicked, the eternal happiness of the righteous, and the eternity of God, as far as Revelation is concerned, form the same building. The Univeralist has placed his shoulders against the basement pillars, and if he succeeds the whole structure falls; but he and his co-laborers may toil and sweat, and leave their bones to molder away in the cellars, but God lives on, the righteous shout on, and the damned groan on — throughout all eternity — O Eternity!

"The meaning of such a word in its connection with the future punishment of the wicked is dreadful — O Eternity! Its significance is as high and wide and deep and grand as God is. He fills it, and it fills Him, and all the worlds, and all the men, and all the demons, and all the angels, but perform their parts in its awful shadow." (*Eternal Retribution*, p. 61)

F — FILTHINESS

"He that is unjust, let him be unjust still: and he which is *filthy*, let him be *filthy* still: and he that is holy, let him be holy still" (Revelation 22:11).

God looked down from Heaven to see if there were any that understood and here is what He saw: "They are all gone aside, they are all together become *filthy*: there is none that doeth good, no not one." (Psalm 14:2,3). Job speaks of man and asks, "How much more abominable and *filthy* is man, which drinketh iniquity like water?" (Job 15:16), and Isaiah says of man, "But we are as an unclean thing, and all our righteousnesses are as *filthy* rags" (Isaiah 64:6). People are said to be filthy in this life and if they die unsaved they go to a place of filthiness forever. Hee are some of the filthy people who will be in hell: "But the fearful and unbelieving, and the abominable, and murderers, and whoremongers, and sorcerers,

45

and idolaters, and all liars, shall have their part in the lake which burneth with fire and brimstone: which is the second death" (Revelation 21:8).

"Know ye not that the unrighteous shall not inherit the kingdom of God? Be not deceived: neither fornicators, nor idolaters, nor adulterers, nor effeminate, nor abusers of themselves with mankind, Nor thieves, nor covetous, nor drunkards, nor revilers, nor extortioners, shall inherit the kingdom of God" (I Corinthians 6:9,10).

What a list of companions of those who go to Hell: people who are fearful, unbelieving, abominable, murderers, whoremongers, sorcerers, idolaters, liars, fornicators, adulterers, effeminate, homosexuals, thieves, covetous, drunkards, revilers, extortioners.

J. Wilbur Chapman tells the story of an unsaved girl who had a Christian father. Once the two were riding the train together. The father stepped out of the car for a moment, and the girl was surrounded by young men who were using profanity, and taking God's name in vain, using all sorts of vulgarity. It shocked her to hear what they had to say, to hear them blaspheme the Name of God. When her father returned to the coach, she said, "Father, let's get out of here immediately." They went into another car and sat down, and the girl leaned her head on her father's shoulder and began to weep and said, "Oh, Father, how vulgar and profane they were. I just couldn't stand it another minute. I am so glad to get out of there." The father said, "Daughter, do you realize that is the kind of people who are going to Hell? You're an unsaved girl, and you're lost and you're going to Hell too. And that is the kind of people you are going to spent eternity with." She said, "Oh, my Father, tell me once more how to be saved, and I will trust the Lord Jesus. I don't want to go to Hell. I don't want to be in Hell with that kind of people."

G — GLOOM

The word "gloom" means "a partial or total darkness; a dark place; an atmosphere of despondency."

Nahum speaks of the goodness of the Lord to those who trust Him, but then He says of those who do not trust Him, "darkness shall pursue his [God's] enemies" (Nahum 1:7-8). God, in speaking of the wicked, says, "Wherefore their ways shall be unto them as slippery ways in the darkness; they shall be driven on and fall therein" (Jeremiah 23:12). Solomon wrote, "For there shall be no reward to the evil man; the candle of the wicked shall be put out" (Proverbs 24:20). God warns: "Hear ye, and give ear; be not proud: for the LORD hath spoken. Give glory to the LORD your God, before he cause darkness, and before your feet stumble upon the dark mountains, and, while ye look for light, he turn it into the shadow of death, and make it gross darkness" (Jeremiah 13:15,16).

Someone has written of the gloom of a lost soul:

LOST IN ETERNITY'S GLOOM

O, what an awful word! *Lost souls.* Can you get a faint idea of the measureless depth of meaning in the two small words? What oceans of tears! What overwhelming bursts of wailing and gnashing of teeth! What eternities of despair! Irredeemably lost! No chance for a light to shine out on their devil-begirt, furnace-heated, pall-shrouded, downward, outward, hellward pathway. Lost to happiness and holiness! Lost to God and the redeemed! Lost to heaven and hope. Lost, and no hope of ever being found. Not one dim, distant hope of ever being anything but more hopelessly, ruinously, despairingly lost, during all the eternities to come.

From woe to more woe; misery to worse misery; ever always lost! Lost because they would be lost. Lost, while their bosom friend was found. Lost, while Jesus was seeking them, and found them lost; but they would not be found. They might have been found, but would not. They gained the world and lost their souls. They gained the shadow and lost the substance; gained the briers and lost the flowers; gained famine and lost plenty; gained foes and lost a Friend; gained eternal damnation and lost eternal life.

Lost amid outer darkness! Lost in the smoke of torment! Lost in the lake of fire and brimstone! Lost amid the howlings of myriads of tormenting devils, the shrieks of the damned, and horrible tempest, the thousand thun-

ders! Lost! Lost!! Lost!!! The bells of eternity are tolling
the requiem. Time warned you. The Bible warned you.
The Judgment and providences of God warn you. The
Spirit warned you. Shall you and your loved ones be lost?
Decide now while Jesus calls, or you are lost.

Lost to earth's pleasures that once thy soul won.
Lost earth's fond friendship to sorrow alone,
Lost amid ruined hopes ever undone;
Lost! the enchantment is o'er.
Lost where the billows of torment e'er roll;
Lost where God's wrath flame envelops the soul;
Lost where no gleam of hope comes to console,
Lost in eternity's gloom.

H — HOPELESSNESS

The Bible says, "When a wicked man dieth, his expectation shall perish: and the *hope of unjust men
perisheth*" (Proverbs 11:7), and "the hope of the
righteous shall be gladness: but *the expectation of the
wicked shall perish*" (Proverbs 10:28). Another verse
that says almost the same thing is Proverbs 14:32: "The
wicked is driven away in his wickedness: but the
righteous hath hope in his death."

Paul writes of the unsaved: "That at that time ye were
without Christ, being aliens from the commonwealth of
Israel, and strangers from the covenants of promise,
having *no hope*, and without God in the world:"
(Ephesians 2:12).

Dante has written over the portal of Hell: "Relinquish
all hope, ye who enter here."

Dr. L. R. Scarborough writes of a man who died
without hope. In a sermon he tells the story:

DYING WITHOUT HOPE

In my pastorate at Abilene years ago in a great revival
which I was holding in my church, I went as my custom
was to see the people. I went to the office and invited the
proprietor who had just come to the town to make our
church his church home. He was a big, fine-looking man.
He looked me in the face and said, "Are you the pastor of
that church?" I said, "I am;" and for two or three minutes I

stood and heard him swear and curse preachers and churches and Christians. Then he walked back into the private room of his hotel. During that meeting God led back from twenty-seven years of backsliding, led there by this wicked man, his wife. I led to Christ his son, who now, thank God, is preaching the gospel in California. I led to Christ his daughter who is a student in our Training School at Fort Worth. When that meeting was over, one day my telephone rang. That wife at the other end of the line said, "Come." I went to that hotel. I went into that family room. There stood the weeping wife and the sorrowing children. There lay that big strong man on his bed breathing his last. He had been suddenly taken with an incurable disease. His lips moved and his wife said, "Put your ear to his lips and hear what he says." I am sorry I did. A thousand times his dying words have rung in my soul — "Dying without hope; dying without God; dying without Christ — hopeless, hopeless!" For twenty-five times, I guess, his strength enabled him to say it; and then he went out into eternity.

I want to tell you while you're living, God says you are without Christ and without hope if you have never trusted Jesus Christ as your Saviour. (*Prepare to Meet God*, pp. 24-26).

I — INDIGNATION

God's Word clearly states: "But unto them that are contentious, and do not obey the truth, but obey unrighteousness, *indignation* and wrath, tribulation and anguish, upon every soul of man that doeth evil, of the Jew first, and also of the Gentile" (Romans 2:8,9).

"But the LORD is the true God, he is the living God, and an everlasting king: at his wrath the earth shall tremble, and the nations shall not be able to abide his *indignation*" (Jeremiah 10:10).

"The same shall drink of the wine of the wrath of God, which is poured out without mixture into the cup of his *indignation*; and he shall be tormented with fire and brimstone in the presence of the holy angels, and in the presence of the Lamb: And the smoke of their torment ascendeth up for ever and ever: and they have no rest day nor night, who worship the beast and his image, and whosoever receiveth the mark of his name" (Revelation 14:10,11).

This indignation is another name for God's wrath, of which we have already written, and here God says that those who experience His indignation "shall be tormented with fire and brimstone . . . and the smoke of their torment ascendeth up for ever and ever."

Joseph Alleine, a much-used preacher of years ago, spoke to the unconverted and warned them: "Now you can put off the evil day, and laugh and be merry, and forget the terror of the Lord. But how will you hold out, or hold up, when God casts you into a 'bed or torments' (Revelation 2:22); and makes you to 'lie down in sorrow' (Isaiah 1:11); when roarings and blasphemies shall be your only music, and the wine of the wrath of God, which is poured out without mixture into the cup of His indignation, shall be your only drink (Revelation 14:10)? In a word, when the smoke of your torment shall ascend for ever and ever, and you shall have no rest day nor night, no rest in your conscience, no rest in your bones; but you shall be an execration, an astonishment, and a curse and a reproach, for evermore (Jeremiah 42:18?" (*An Alarm to the Unconverted*, p. 65).

J — JUDGMENT

God has made it clear in His Word many times that a time of judgment is coming: "Rejoice, O young man, in thy youth: and let thy heart cheer thee in the days of thy youth, and walk in the ways of thine heart, and in the sight of thine eyes: but know thou, that for all these things God will bring thee into judgment" (Ecclesiastes 11:9).

"For God shall bring every work into judgment, with every secret thing, whether it be good, or whether it be evil" (Ecclesiastes 12:14).

"Because he hath appointed a day, in the which he will judge the world in righteousness by that man whom he hath ordained; whereof he hath given assurance unto all men, in that he hath raised him from the dead" (Acts 17:31).

"And as it is appointed unto men once to die, but after this the judgment" (Hebrews 9:27).

When the sentence is passed upon the unsaved at the great white throne judgment, all of them will be cast into the lake of fire (Revelation 20:11-15). The Bible speaks of "eternal judgment" (Hebrews 6:2) and Hell is God's place of eternal judgment against sin.

K — KEEPING

Hell is a place of keeping — where the wicked will be kept for all eternity. Dr. Harry Ironside spoke of this place of imprisonment: "Hell is God's well-ordered prison house; the lake of fire is His penitentiary."

Evangelist Fred Barlow commented on Hell as a place of unescapable doom:

Criminals behind the bars, sentenced for life and even for execution, live in hope that they may be paroled, escape, get to freedom someday, someway.

Some succeed. In my file I have a clipping of a newspaper account of a jail break in Doylestown, Pennsylvania:

Bucks County prison officials reported the most amazing escape they ever encountered. Warden Earl D. Handy said Robert Henderson, 22-year-old Philadelphian held on a car theft charge, apparently used a small piece of steel from an old lock and several short lengths of lumber to:

1. Break out of his solitary confinement cell.
2. Smash through a steal mesh grating.
3. Break the panes of a closely leaded window.
4. Squeeze his 170 pounds through a space five-and-one-half by thirteen inches he had sprung between two one-inch bars.
5. Scale a ten-foot wall and barb-wire fence.
6. Climb over a thirty-one foot wall.

But Hell is not a penitentiary from which a person can ever escape or ever hope for release. For God does not consign a soul to Hell to make him penitent for sin and to rehabilitate him for a heavenly society someday. God

51

sends a sinner to Hell to punish him for committing the unrepentable, unforgivable sin — the final and eternal rejection of Christ (Revelation 20:11-15)." (*Dead Men Tell Tales*, pp. 12-13).

L — LAKE OF FIRE

Five times in the Bible the lake of fire is mentioned: Revelation 19:20; 20:10; 20:14; 20:15; 21:8. Fire is used many times in the New Testament in reference to Hell:

"hewn down and cast into the *fire*" — Matthew 3:10; 7:19; Luke 3:9.

"he will burn up the chaff with unquenchable *fire*" — Matthew 3:12.

"whosoever shall say, Thou fool, shall be in danger of hell *fire*" — Matthew 5:22.

"the tares are gathered and burned in the *fire*; so shall it be in the end of this world" — Matthew 13:40.

"And shall cast them into a furnace of *fire*" — Matthew 13:42,50.

"having two hands or two feet to be cast into hell *fire*" — Matthew 18:8.

"having two eyes to be cast into hell *fire*" — Matthew 18:9; Mark 9:47.

"Depart from me, ye cursed, into everlasting *fire*" — Matthew 25:41.

"to go into hell, into the *fire* that never shall be quenched" — Mark 9:43.

"the *fire* is not quenched" — Mark 9:44,46,48.

"cast into hell, into the *fire* that never shall be quenched" — Mark 9:45.

"the chaff he will burn with *fire* unquenchable — Luke 3:17.

"in flaming *fire* taking vengeance on them that know not God" — II Thessalonians 1:8.

"it is set on *fire* of hell" — James 3:6.

"suffering the vengeance of eternal *fire*" — Jude 7.

"he shall be tormented with *fire* and brimstone" — Revelation 14:10.

"cast alive into the lake of *fire*" — Revelation 19:20.

"the devil that deceived them was cast into the lake of *fire*" — Revelation 20:10.

"And death and hell were cast into the lake of *fire*" — Revelation 20:14.

"And whosoever was not found written in the book of life was cast into the lake of *fire*" — Revelation 20:15.

"shall have their part in the lake which burneth with *fire* and brimstone" — Revelation 21:8.

Robert Ripley, in his "Believe It or Not" column, stated, "Believe it or not, there is not enough combustible material in the universe to supply an everlasting fire. Therefore, there will be no such fire!" Professor C. T. Schwarze, of New York University, member of the American Association for the Advancement of Science, on a radio broadcast conducted by Erling C. Olsen over station WMCA, New York City, stated that, according to Matthew 25:41: "Depart from me, ye cursed, into everlasting fire, prepared for the devil and his angels," the fire is already in existence. He said that the Greek word translated "prepared" in this verse is *hetoimazo*, which means "already prepared," or "now ready," and he also said that this fire is not a fire of combustible materials. Professor Schwarze writes:

"The word *lake* must connote a body of matter having liquid form. Therefore, if Scripture is true, this eternal fire must be in liquid form.

". . . the very simple proof of the portions of Scripture we have been discussing *lies in the existence of the singular phenomena of the skies known as midget or white dwarf stars!*. . . .

a. A midget star is one which, because of some things which have happened to it (not quite clear at this time), should be roughly 5,000 times or more *times* as big as it really is! Applying this idea for illustration to such a planet as the earth, you must conceive the earth as having shrunk to such an extent that its diameter would be about 400 miles . . . instead of being 8,000 miles in diameter as it really is.

"This enormous density . . . has a great deal to do with our subject. . . . Most people know the sun, or nearest star is rather hot . . . there is general agreement that the temperature at or near the center of stars is between 25 million and 30 million degrees Fahrenheit! . . . at such temperatures, much can happen, like the bursting of atoms, which helps to explain the phenomenon of the white dwarf. . . .

* * *

". . . a temperature of 30,000,000 degrees Fahrenheit could explode atoms. . . .

"It would cause the atoms to lose their electrons even though the attraction between nucleus and electrons is an octillion . . . times the attraction of gravity. The separated parts could then be better packed in, particularly under such great pressure. . . . With the constant activity of X-rays, atom walls could not be reformed; therefore enormous densities, such as are found in the midgets, can be attained. Now, please note, at such high temperatures all matter would be in the form of gas . . . in a white dwarf the pressure is so great that gases become compressed to the consistency of a liquid although they may still respond to the characteristics of a gas. . . .

* * *

". . . Before such a star could cool off and gradually become dark, it would have to expand to normal proportions. That is, it would have to get to be more than 5,000 times its present size. Here's the difficulty. Such expansion would cause enormous heat, which, in turn, would absolutely keep the star compressed, so that, *insofar as astronomers and physicists know, the midget stars can never cool off!* . . . The white dwarf, to all intents, *can never burn out.*

". . . may I summarize to show that the Bible, God's Word, is scientifically accurate? We find, first, an eternal fire which cannot burn out. Because of a liquid consistency it is, secondly, a lake of fire. In the third place, it cannot be quenched, for any quenching material, such as water, would immediately have its atoms stripped of electrons and be packed in with the rest. In the fourth place, since astronomers have been, and still are, studying this strange phenomena, it is only too evident that the lake of fire *has been prepared* and is now ready.

Although we cannot say that God will actually use

54

these lakes of fire in fulfilling His Word, the answer to the skeptic is in the heavens where there *are* lakes of fires. . . ." ("The Bible and Science on the Everlasting Fire," *Bibliotheca Sacra*, 95:105-112, January, 1938).

Robert L. Summer speaks of real fire in Hell:

Do not misunderstand me, there is a *real* Hell or *real* fire which makes sinners grit their teeth for pain, cry out for water, and beg for mercy! Jude 7 says, "Even as Sodom and Gomorrah, and the cities about them in like manner, giving themselves over to fornication, and going after strange flesh, are set forth for an example, suffering the vengeance of eternal fire." Since it was *real* fire and *real* brimstone which destroyed Sodom and Gomorrah — and that was just a sample of Hell — we can expect *real* fire and *real* brimstone in the eternal land of the lost." (*Hell Is No Joke*, p. 32).

Fred Brown comments: "The question always comes, will the fire of hell be real fire. Yes, it will be more terrible than fire we know. Fire here can destroy the body without touching the soul. There, it punishes the body without destroying it and at the same time punishes the soul.

"I would rather try to keep people out of hell than to argue about the kind of fire, but whatever it is, it is fire and those flames will burn forever, and the waves of that 'lake of fire' will splash forever against those precipitous shores." (*The Biblical Faith of Baptists*, Book 3, p. 212).

John F. Walvoord in his book, *The Revelation of Jesus Christ*, speaks of the lake of fire:

Many attempts have been made to escape the obvious meaning of this passage by spiritualizing the lake of fire as a mere symbol that is not as bad as it seems, or, on the other hand, to represent it as the annihilation of the wicked rather than the beginning of their eternal punishment. It may be conceded that the lake of fire is a symbol, but the symbol corresponds to reality. The rich man in Luke 16 gave his testimony: "I am tormented in this flame" (Luke 16:24). If unsaved souls in Hades, the intermediate state, are tormented by flames, it is not unreasonable to assume that the lake of fire connotes the same type of punishment. It cannot safely be assumed that there is any important difference between the physical and the spiritual reality embodied in the term "lake of fire". It is an awful destiny in either case. (p. 309).

William Evans answers the question of whether there will be literal fire in this lake of fire:

> It is contended that fire must necessarily consume; that nothing could continue to exist in fire. Is it not remarkable that the Baptist [John] uses the word "unquenchable" (Greek, "asbestos") when speaking of this fire? Is any light thrown on the question by the incident of the three Hebrew children in the fiery furnace? Did they consume, or did they withstand the fire? (Daniel 3:27). In the parable of the Tares (Matthew 13:36-43) our Lord speaks of the tares being burned up. When Christ returned to the house after delivering the parable, His disciples asked Him what He meant by the figures of speech He used in the parable. This request He granted. He explained the figurative language of the parable; every figurative word in it except that of "fire". He said: "The field is the world; the good seed are the seed of the kingdom; but the tares are the children of the wicked one; the enemy that sowed them is the devil; the harvest is the end of the world; and the reapers are the angels. As therefore the tares are gathered and burned in the fire, so shall it be at the end of this world. . . . And they shall cast them into a furnace of fire: there shall be wailing and gnashing of teeth." Why did not the Master explain what He meant by the figurative word "fire"? He explained all the other figurative words, why not this one? Did He forget? Or did He intend that His deisciples should have the impression that He was speaking of literal fire? Here was His opportunity to explain His use of words, for the disciples were asking for just that very thing. Was there any significance in the fact that Jesus did not explain the word "fire"? Whether He believed in literal fire or not, we certainly ought to ask for a reason for the Master's failure to literalize the figurative word "fire". (*The Great Doctrines of the Bible*, p. 262).

John Holliday in his message, "Final Judgment and Eternal Hell," also spoke of fire:

> Any effort to soften the Bible doctrine of hell by making the fire figurative is utterly futile. According to

Jesus, both body and soul are involved in the miseries of hell (Matthew 10:28) and from His unveilings of the remorse and retribution to be endured, the flames that sear the soul are more terrible than the fires that scorch the body. (*The Biblical Faith of Baptists*, pp. 157-158).

Robert G. Gromacki wrote concerning the lake of fire:

Actually, there is no good reason to deny the literalness of the lake of fire. If real, resurrected bodies will go into a real heaven, then a real Satan, real fallen angels, and real bodies of the lost will go into a real place, called the lake of fire.

How can a human body live in a sea of fire without being consumed in a few minutes? The natural bodies we now inhabit could not survive, but remember the unsaved are going to receive new bodies. They will not be glorified bodies, fashioned to the image of Jesus Christ, but they will be of such a composition that they will be able to endure forever the fiery torments without being destroyed. God preserved the three Hebrew children in the midst of Nebuchadnezzar's furnace (Daniel 3). The intermediate body of the rich man did not perish in the torment of hell (Luke 16). So it will be in the lake of fire. God will match the fire with the resurrected body of the unsaved. (*Are These the Last Days*, pp. 185-86).

Dr. John R. Rice in his excellent sermon "Is There Literal Physical Fire in Hell?", concluded:

Verses 14 and 15 of this 20th chapter of Revelation read: "And death and hell were cast into the lake of fire. This is the second death. And whosoever was not found written in the book of life was cast into the lake of fire."

This is a punishment for people with resurrected bodies. And with physical bodies these people will be cast into the lake of fire. If the resurrection is literal, then Hell is literal. If the bodies are physical bodies, then Hell is a physical Hell. If the judgment is literal, then why should not the fire and brimstone be literal? Hell is a lake of fire!

* * *

I think I know why Paul went about weeping, "night and day with tears" (Acts 20:31), when he so believed in a literal Hell of eternal fire and torment! I beg of you who read this, become consumed with the passion to save people from Hell! We may be fundamental in our heads, but most of us are partly infidels in our hearts, for we have no real conception of the wickedness of sin, and we have no real conception of the marvel of God's love and His infinite grace expressed at Calvary! Most of us have no sense of the awfulness of sin and the certain, horrible doom of Christ-rejecting sinners!

Oh, brother, let us win souls while we may to keep them from the lake of fire, that awful place burning with brimstone, prepared for the Devil and his angels! (*Twelve Tremendous Themes*, pp. 185,188).

When I began this study of Hell, I had always thought that the fire in Hell is literal. Many of the writers whom I have checked, some of them good Bible-believing men, think that the fire in Hell is figurative. My study of the subject has confirmed my belief that there will be literal fire in a literal place and that those who go there will have their literal bodies which will never burn up — neither will the fire of Hell burn out. God, Who is able to burn a bush without its being consumed (Exodus 3:2), and Who can keep three bodies in a fire without their being consumed (Daniels 3:21-27), is also able to give the unrepentant sinner a body of such a composition that it will be able to endure the fiery torments of Hell for all eternity without being destroyed. Munsey's statement is appropriate here: "The Hell of the Bible is horrible beyond description, and the hypotheses of this hour cannot exceed it. Its miseries are as far beyond description as the joys of heaven are. Be it better or worse, oh let us not go there!" (*Eternal Retribution*, p. 78).

M — MEMORY

Hell is a place of memory. The rich man in Hell was told by Abraham, "Son, remember" (Luke 16:25). Psychologists today agree that we never forget anything, and a report was given to the American Psychiatric Institute in Montreal some time ago of how nerves store memory and an electrical way to remember what you forget. Using fine wires, with a slight electrical current touching human brain structures during a brain operation, Dr. Walker Penfield, head of McGill University Neurological Institute in Montreal, stated, "The probes drew forth old and forgotten memories almost like taking cards from a filing case."

In commenting on the rich man in Hell, Dr. G. Beauchamp Vick, pastor of the Temple Baptist Church, of Detroit, Michigan, wrote:

Oh, my friends, memory has been called the storehouse of the soul. What did Abraham tell him to remember? The things that happened in his lifetime.

"Son, remember that thou in thy lifetime receivedst thy good things, and likewise Lazarus evil things; but now he is comforted and thou are tormented". "Son, remember". Yes, the memory that you will retain in Hell will be one of the awful horrors of that eternal inferno. Remember the good things, the good opportunities which you enjoyed in your lifetime. Those wasted opportunities of years gone by. "Son, remember" how God let you be born in the land of open Bibles; in a land of open churches, in a land where the Gospel was just as near you as the radio or television dial in your living room, if you wanted to hear it. "Son, remember" how a fellow by the name of Beauchamp Vick spoke to you week after week warning you to flee from the wrath of God to come. How he repeatedly told you of the horrors of an eternal hell for every soul that rejects Christ. Remember every church service that you attended. Remember that God has sent preachers of all kinds your way, yet you said "no" to it all.

Remember every Gospel message which God let you hear, and yet you said "no" to it all.

Remember every personal worker who pled with you to receive the Lord Jesus Christ and repent of your sins, but you said "no" to it all.

Remember every prayer of a godly Christian mother.

Remember every prayer of all your friends which you ignored.

Yes, my friends, some of you will remember every invitation hymn which you rejected.

You will remember every Gospel invitation to which you said, "no".

You will remember time after time when you sat as the claims of Jesus Christ were being pressed home upon your soul and you hardened your heart, you stiffened your neck and you said, "no" to it all.

"Son, remember, that thou in thy lifetime receivedst thy good things, and likewise Lazarus evil things; but now he is comforted, and thou are tormented". (Sermon, "What the Bible Says About Hell," pp. 12-13).

N — NO REST

"The same shall drink of the wine of the wrath of God, which is poured out without mixture into the cup of his indignation; and he shall be tormented with fire and brimstone in the presence of the holy angels, and in the presence of the Lamb: And the smoke of their torment ascendeth up for ever and ever: and they have no rest day nor night, who worship the beast and his image, and whosoever receiveth the mark of his name" (Revelation 14:10,11).

The Bible says that those who are unsaved have no rest in this life: "But the wicked are like the troubled sea, when it cannot rest, whose waters cast up mire and dirt. There is no peace, saith my God, to the wicked" (Isaiah 57:20,21). Those dying in their sins will have no rest throughout eternity. Jesus promises: "Come unto me, all ye that labour and are heavy laden, and I will give you rest. Take my yoke upon you, and learn of me; for I am meek and lowly in heart: and ye shall find rest unto your souls. For my yoke is easy, and my burden is light" (Matthew 11:28-30). Those who do not come to Jesus and receive Him as Saviour and Lord will be restless in life and in eternity.

Oswald J. Smith tells a true story about "The Hell Club":

More than a century ago there was in Glasgow a club of gentlemen of the first rank in that city. They met professedly for card playing, but the members were distinguished by such a fearless excess of sin as to obtain the name of "The Hell Club."

Besides their nightly or weekly meetings, they held a grand annual festival, at which each member endeavored to outdo his comrades in drunkenness, blasphemy, and licentiousness. Of them all on these occasions, none was so reckless as Archibald Boyle.

One night, on retiring to sleep after returning from one of the annual meetings, Boyle dreamt that he was still riding, as usual, upon his famous black horse, towards his own house, and that he was suddenly approached by someone whose personal appearance, he could not, in the gloom of the night, distinctly discern, but who, seizing the reins, said, in a voice apparently accustomed to command: "You must go with me".

"And who are you?" exclaimed Boyle, with a volley of curses, while he struggled to disengage his reins from the intruder's grasp.

"That you will see by and by," replied the same voice, in a cold, sneering tone that chilled Boyle's heart.

Boyle plunged his spurs into the panting sides of his steed. It fiercely reared and plunged — he lost his seat, and expected at the moment to feel himself dashed to the earth. But not so, for he continued to fall — fall — fall with an ever-increasing velocity.

At length this terrific rapidity of motion abated, and, to his amazement and horror, he perceived that his mysterious attendant was close by his side.

"Where," he exclaimed, in the frantic energy of despair, "where are you taking me — where am I — where am I going?"

"To hell", replied the same iron voice, and, from the depths below, the sound so familiar to his lips was re-echoed.

Onward they hurried in darkness until they reached it. Multitudes were there, gnashing their teeth in the hopelessness of mad despair, cursing the day that gave them birth.

There sat his former friend, Mrs. Dell, with her eyes fixed in intense earnestness, as she was wont on earth, apparently absorbed in her favorite game of loo.

Boyle addressed her, "Come now, my good Mrs. Dell, for auld lang syne, do just stop for a moment's rest".

With a shriek that seemed to cleave through his very

61

soul, she exclaimed — 'Rest! there is no rest in hell!' And from interminable vaults, voices as loud as thunder, repeated the awful, the heart-withering sound, "There is no rest in hell".

"Take me", shrieked Boyle, "take me from this place! By the living God, whose name I have so often outraged, I adjure thee, take me from this place".

"Canst thou still name His name?" said the fiend, with a hideous sneer; "go, then, but — *in a year and a day we meet to part no more!*"

Boyle awoke, and he felt as if the last words of the fiend were traced in letters of living fire upon his heart and brain.

He resolved, utterly and forever, to forsake "The Club" . . . especially the annual meeting.

Well aware of this resolve, his tempters determined he should have no choice, and so Boyle found himself, he could not tell how, seated at that table, on that very day, where he had sworn to himself a thousand times nothing on earth would make him sit.

His ears tingled as the president remarked, "Gentlemen, this is leap year; therefore it is a *year and a day* since our last annual meeting".

Boyle started at the omnious, the well-remembered words. His first impulse was to rise and fly, but then — the sneers.

The night was gloomy, with frequent and fitful gusts of chill and howling wind, as Boyle, with fevered nerves and reeling brain, mounted his horse to return home.

The following morning the well-known black steed was found, with saddle and bridle on, quietly grazing on the roadside, about halfway to Boyle's country house, and a few yards from it lay the stiffened corpse of its master.

Archibald Boyle's dream is a well-authenticated fact. And God would speak by it to any who, like Boyle, are throwing their life and eternal soul away with reckless abandon. There is a hell, a real hell reserved for all who have never made Jesus Christ Saviour. There is a heaven of glory for those who have put their trust in Him and been born into God's family.

O — OBLIVION

Oblivion means "the state of being blotted out from the memory; a being forgotten." Many times I have been asked the question: "How can anyone be happy in Heaven when some of his loved ones are in Hell?" The Bible teaches that "the righteous shall be in everlasting remembrance" (Psalm 112:6), but it also teaches that those who go to Hell will be forgotten by their loved ones in Heaven. "Drought and heat consume the snow waters: so doth the grave those which have sinned. The womb shall forget him; the worm shall feed sweetly on him; he shall be no more remembered; and wickedness shall be broken as a tree" (Job 24:19,20).

Notice, verse 20 says of the wicked: "The womb [the mother] shall forget him [the sinner] . . . he shall be no more remembered." The lost sinner in Hell will be completely forgotten by those who are in Heaven — they will be blotted out from the memory.

"The wicked shall be turned into hell, and all the nations that forget God" (Psalm 9:17). Those who have forgotten God will be forgotten by those who are with Him.

P — PAIN

Four times in the story of the rich man in Hell we are told of the torment he suffered: "And in hell he lift up his eyes, being in *torments* . . .; I am *tormented* in this flame . . . thou are *tormented* . . . this place of *torment*" (Luke 16:23-25,28). In Revelation 14:11 we read, "And the smoke of their *torment* ascendeth up for ever and ever . . ." People in Hell will have no respite from pain — it will be day and night forever and ever. Here people who suffer pain can get relief through drugs and sleep, but in Hell there will be no drugs and no sleep. There will be no end to their pain of body and soul. R. A. Torrey said, "Friends, hell is the hospital of the incurables of the universe, where men exist in awful and perpetual pain" (*Real Salvation*, p. 47).

Evangelist Fred Barlow speaks of the pain in Hell: "How horrible Hell must be! As a pastor for fifteen years I have visited in hospitals. There I have heard the groaning, moaning, sighing, dying patients. I remember a man who was bleeding to death after a rubber mill accident. He had slipped at his machine and had fallen so that his hand and arm had gotten entangled in the whirring razor-sharp knives that had literally 'skinned' him. As he was brought into the ward, I saw him take his mutilated limb and tear the Venetian blinds from the window. He flailed nurses with blows like Joe Louis savagely threw at his opponents in the ring. I saw burly interns, like pro-football linemen, vigorously drive this man into submission, however. They finally harnessed his flailing arms at his side, and then I saw a nurse again and again shoot drugs into his pain-wracked body. Only after a long, long time shrieks of this poor man turned into cries; the cries lowered to moans; the moans ebbed to sobs. He was drugged, knocked out, unconscious! He was living a nightmare, but not realizing the fierce pain, the torments. I bowed my head. I quietly thanked God I was not going to Hell.

" 'Why do you say that, Preacher?' someone asks. Hear me! One reason is there are no drugs in Hell to give relief and release from suffering and torment. There are no nurses, no loved ones to smoth back your rumpled hair, to soothe your burning brow with a loving hand or a moist, cool cloth. There will be no one in Hell to whisper, 'I love you'. There will be no one to care, no one to bear, no one to share your eternal heartache and heartbreak." (*Dead Men Tell Tales*, pp. 7-8).

Q — QUANDRY

Quandry means "a state of difficulty, perplexity, uncertainty, or hesitation; a predicament." Surely, Hell will be all of this, and more. "The sinners in Zion are afraid; fearfulness hath surprised the hypocrites. Who among us shall dwell with the devouring fire? who among us shall dwell with everlasting burnings?" (Isaiah 33:14). Here God speaks of those who "dwell with the devouring fire . . . with everlasting burnings."

Someone has written as if he were in Hell and of his quandry:

> I have told you, my friend, how continuously I am the prey of memories, but how much so — to what extent, I mean — you little guess. That deeds of iniquity and particular sins should assail me, tormenting the soul as with fire, is natural. But this is not all. There are other things, counted for little in the world, which cling to conscience with a terrible vividness. Every little falsehood and unjust dealing, every word of deceit and breach of fealty, every evil example and want of kindness, — they are all, all present now, piercing the heart as with daggers of regret. I thought so little of these things in life, that I scarcely stopped to consider them; they seemed buried on the spot, every year adding its own share to the mouldering heap. They have risen now and stand about me, I see them and I tremble.

> But not mere deeds — every word of evil carelessly spoken in the days of early life comes back to me with similar force. As poisoned arrows such words once quitted my lips; as poisoned arrows they come back to me, piercing the heart. Oh, consider it while living voice is yours, and speak not lightly! There is no saying what harvest of sin may spring from a single word. And if pity for others will not restrain you, be advised by pity for your own selves, since requital will come to yourselves only in the end.

> And not merely deed and words, but every harmful thought recurs to me, to gnaw away at my heart. There is a saying with certain philosophers in the world that nothing ever is lost. If this be true in the material world, how much more so is it in spiritual things — ah, terrible truth!

> And further, apart from the evil done, it is the good left undone, the opportunities wasted, which stand around me with pitiless scourge, and their name is legion! Thus everything, you see, both what I have done and left undone, comes to life here in this place of woe, — takes shape, I ought to say, — rising in accusation against me. I try to escape, but they are about me everywhere, those shapes of terror, enough to people a world with despair;

they persecute me, they torture me, and I am their helpless prey. Memories of the good left undone — alas, they are far more bitter than those of the evil done! For temptation to do wrong often was great, and in my own strength I failed to conquer; but to do good for the most part would have cost little, if any, effort. I see it now with the new insight into life which hell gives. The man lives not who is excused from leaving good undone; however poor and humbly situated he may be, opportunity is ever at his door. It is for him only to open his heart and take in the opportunity; for his own heart is a well of power and of blessing to boot. He who is the fountain of love and purity, from whom every good and perfect gift cometh, has wondrously arranged it, that in this respect there is but little difference between the rich and the poor, the gentle and the simple. Let me conjure you then, brothers and sisters, listen to the voice of your heart while yet it is day! Listen, I say, and obey, lest the bitterness of repentance overtake you with the night, when no man can work! Ah, let no opportunity for the doing of good escape you, for it will rise against you when nothing is left but to wail in anguish. (*The Lost Soul's First Day in Eternity,* pp. 97-98, 99-102).

R — RETRIBUTION

Hell is a place of retribution, where God will give to every unsaved person exactly what he deserves. God says, "But he that doeth wrong shall receive for the wrong which he hath done: and there is no respect of persons" (Colossians 3:25).

"Now will I shortly pour out my fury upon thee, and accomplish mine anger upon thee: and I will judge thee according to thy ways, and will recompense thee for all thine abominations. And mine eye shall not spare, neither will I have pity: I will recompense thee according to thy ways and thine abominations that are in the midst of thee; and ye shall know that I am the LORD that smiteth" (Ezekiel 7:8-9).

"Seeing it is a righteous thing with God to recompense tribulation to them that trouble you; And to you who are troubled rest with us, when the Lord Jesus shall be revealed from heaven with his mighty angels, In flaming fire taking vengeance on them that know not God, and that obey not the gospel of our Lord Jesus Christ: Who shall be punished with everlasting destruction from the presence of the Lord, and from the glory of his power" (II Thessalonians 1:6-9).

S — SHAME

In speaking of the resurrection, the Bible says: "And many of them that sleep in the dust of the earth shall awake, some to everlasting life, and some to shame and everlasting contempt" (Daniel 12:2).

Some (the unsaved) shall awake to shame and everlasting contempt.

Dr. R. A. Torrey tells the true story of what shame can cause:

In America, in New York State, we had a bank cashier in a bank, who was in a hurry to get rich, so he appropriated the funds of the bank and invested them, intending to pay them back. But his investment was a failure. For a long time he kept the books so as to blind the bank examiner, but one day when the bank examiner was going over the books he detected the embezzlement. He called in the cashier — he had to acknowledge his defalcation. He was arrested, tried, and sent to the State's prison. He had a beautiful wife and lovely child, a sweet angel-like little girl. Sometime after his arrest and imprisonment, the little child came home sobbing with a breaking heart. "Oh," she said, "Mother, I can never go back to that school again. Send for my books." "Oh," she said, "My darling," thinking it was some childish whim, "of course you will go back." "No," she said, "Mother, I can never go back. Send for my books." She said, "Darling, what is the matter?" She said, "Another little girl said to me today, 'Your father is a thief'." Oh, the cruel stab! The mother saw that she could not go back to school. The wound was fatal. That fair blossom began to fade. A physician was called in, but it surpassed all the capacities of his art. The child faded and faded, until they laid her upon her bed, and the physician said, "Madam, I must tell you this is a case in which I am powerless; the child's heart has given way with the agony of the wound. Your child must die." The mother went in and said to her dying child, "Darling, is there anything you would like to have me do for you?" "Oh," she said, "yes, Mother, send for Father. Let him come home, and lay his head down on the pillow beside mine as he used to do." Ah! but that was just what could not be done. The father was behind iron bars. They sent to the governor of the State, and he said, "I have no power in the matter." They sent to the warden of the prison. He said, "I have no power in the matter."

But hearts were so touched that they got the judge and every member of the jury and the governor, and they got up a petition, and they made arrangements whereby the father was suffered to come home under a deputy-warden. He reached his home late at night, entered his house. The physician was waiting. He said, "I think you had better go in tonight, for I am afraid your child will not live till morning." The father went to the door and opened it. The child looked quickly up. "Oh," she said, "I knew it was you, Father. I knew you would come. Father, come and lay your head beside mine upon the pillow just as you used to do." And the strong man went and laid his head upon the pillow, and the child lovingly patted his cheek, and died. Killed by shame. Men and women, hell is the place of shame, where everybody is dishonored. (*Real Salvation*, pp. 51-52).

T — THIRST

The rich man in Hell begged for water. "And he cried and said, Father Abraham, have mercy on me, and send Lazarus, that he may dip the tip of his finger in water, and cool my tongue; for I am tormented in this flame" (Luke 16:24). He wanted even one drop of water.

Evangelist Fred Barlow tells an interesting story about thirst:

Oh, the terrible thirsting in Hell! Nothing can compare with it. The account of the Battle of Dardanelles, written by an English lieutenant during the first World War, cannot begin to describe the sufferings of sinners in Hell. In *A Thousand Dollars for A Drop*, the author tells how his men, marooned on shore, could not reach their ship in safety. In a short time their canteens were empty. Desperately they tried to slake their thirst with sea-water but this made matters worse. Next, they lay down and put their tongues upon the damp sand, but this, too, had too much salt. Parched-tongued, some took off their shoes and ate on them to get a little moisture. Their one great cry was, "Water! Water! Water! Give me a drop! A thousand dollars for a drop!" Many went mad with thirst and blew out their brains. Others begged for water and fainted, some to die of thirst, their tongues protruding out of their mouths. The correspondent said that the sight and groans were so awful that if Hell could be worse, "Good Lord, save me from Hell."

Hell is worse! For lost souls not only crave a drop of water to satisfy their thirst, they crave their sin. For everyone who goes to Hell goes there because he preferred sin to the Saviour. . . .

If this lost soul in our text would have thirsted for Christ, "The Water of Life," when he was alive, he would have been satisfied and saved from Hell, for the Saviour calls sinners, "Whosoever drinketh of the water that I shall give him shall never thirst; but the water that I shall give him shall be in him a well of water springing up into everlasting life" (John 4:14). But because he thirsted for sin, nineteen hundred years later he is still craving, seeking for gratification of sin, never to be satisfied. (*Dead Men Tell Tales*, pp. 11-12).

U — UNGODLINESS

The ungodly in this world will go to a place of ungodliness in the next world. The question is asked, "Where shall the *ungodly* and the sinner appear?" (I Peter 4:18). The Psalmist answered, "The *ungodly* are not so, but are like the chaff which the wind driveth away," and "the way of the *ungodly* shall perish" (Psalm 1:4,6).

Dr. Robert P. Shuler tells of an incident which took place when he was a young preacher in Pocahontas, Virginia:

When I was a boy preacher in Virginia, in the days when the little mining towns were literally alive with vice and immorality, when every payday saw murders and crimes of every variety, I recall that late one afternoon a woman called me, asking if I would come to a certain street and pray with a dying girl. I immediately recognized the address as the very heart of the red-light district of that mining village. She said this girl could not live until morning and was calling for a preacher. I told her I would come. I called a fine old man, possibly eighty years of age, asking him if he would go with me on this journey. He agreed. His lovely granddaughter, still in her teens, always played the little organ in the church at the evening services. It was night when we walked up the old board sidewalk. The vile women of the cribs and rooms along the way were in their doors, inviting men to come in. It was a terrible sight. I saw a Negro man and a white woman, with their arms about each other, reel drunkenly down the sidewalk. I think she was the first intoxicated woman I ever saw. The language was filthy. It was my first experience in such an environment. We found the house.

The girl was dying of tuberculosis. She was wasted and spent, yet beautiful. She told a pitiful story. I urged her to save her fast-going strength. But she was bent on telling me how she had been betrayed by one she loved and then disowned by her own mother. The old saint I had brought along wept. We both prayed by her bedside. She prayed. We remained possibly an hour or more. She said that as best she could she had surrendered to Jesus as her Saviour and Lord. Her profession of faith seemed genuine. Her only trouble seemed to be that she could scarcely believe that Jesus would save one who had come to her place and condition. I told her the stories of the woman at the well of Sychar, of Mary Magdalene, of the thief on the cross. There was hope in her eyes. I quoted the "whosoevers." I tried to make it plain — this beautiful path of mercy and forgiveness.

And I am as sure as I am sure I live to preach this Gospel that if that poor penitent child, with her wasted cheeks wet with her tears, gave Jesus her heart that night, she is in a beautiful Heaven even now and her heart is exultant with joy and praise.

As the old man and I walked back down the board sidewalk, the vile picture of a few hours before had quadrupled. I confess that there came over me a kind of sickness. Suddenly I stopped and faced the man who walked with me. "Brother," I said, "did you ever think of your beautiful little granddaughter, who plays the organ down at the church, living forever in a place like this and associating forever with people like these?"

For a moment I thought the old fellow would strike me. He turned deadly white. It was not terror. He went mad.

"What do you mean by that?" he almost hissed.

"I mean that I talked with her only this week, and she told me that she was not a Christian, that she had never accepted Jesus Christ as her personal Saviour. If I know the Book and understand the Gospel message and the plan of salvation and the destiny of those who will not take Jesus as Saviour and Lord, this is the kind of picture of the eternal abode of the lost, its comradeships, its surroundings, its associations."

The old man was pathetic, standing there in the night. He did not answer. He walked silently down the walk. We turned and went by his home. He opened the gate and passed through without speaking to me again that evening.

The next Sunday night the little granddaughter was at the organ in the opening of the service. The old man sat in his place. I preached and made the call. Someone else played the organ in the afterservice, as the old man walked across to that beautiful girl, her eyes brimming with tears, and they came side by side to the altar. He was taking no more chances. He had seen the picture. (Sermon, "The Truth We Will Not Face", *The Sword of the Lord*, November 18, 1966, p. 10).

V — VENGEANCE

God declares: "To me belongeth *vengeance*, and recompense; their foot shall slide in due time: for the day of their calamity is at hand, and the things that shall come upon them make haste" (Deuteronomy 32:35). This is the passage of scripture from which Jonathan Edwards preached his well-known and greatly-used sermon, "Sinners in the Hands of An Angry God." His text was "their foot shall slide in due time."

In this sermon, Jonathan Edwards said: "It is true, that judgment against your evil work has not been executed hitherto; the floods of God's vengeance have been withheld. But your guilt in the meantime is constantly increasing, and you are every day treasuring up more wrath. The waters are continually rising, and waxing more and more mighty; and there is nothing but the mere pleasure of God that holds the waters back, that are unwilling to be stopped, and press hard to go forward.

"If God should only withdraw His hand from the floodgate, it would immediately fly open, and the fiery floods of the fierceness and wrath of God would rush forth with inconceivable fury, and would come upon you with omnipotent power. If your strength were 10,000 times greater than it is, yea 10,000 times greater than the stoutest, sturdiest devil in Hell, it would be nothing to withstand or endure it." (Sermon, "Sinners in the Hands of An Angry God," *Great Sermons by Great Preachers*, pp. 30-31).

"*Vengeance* is mine; I will repay, saith the Lord" (Romans 12:19).

Christ will come again "In flaming fire taking *vengeance* on them that know not God, and that obey not the gospel of our Lord Jesus Christ" (II Thessalonians 1:8).

W — WOE

God's Word pronounces a woe unto the wicked: "Woe unto the wicked! it shall be ill with him: for the reward of his hand shall be given him" (Isaiah 3:11). Jesus said concerning Judas, "*woe* unto that man by whom the Son of man is betrayed! it had been good for that man if he had not been born" (Matthew 26:24). As someone has well said, "Better not to have been born at all than to not have been born again." Someone else has said, "Born once, die twice; born twice, die once."

Catherine Dangell has written a stirring poem entitled

THE HORRORS OF HELL

Hell, the prisonhouse of despair,
Here are some things that won't be there:
No flowers will bloom on the banks of Hell,
No beauties of nature we love so well;
No comforts of home, music and song,
No friendship of joy will be found in that throng;
No children to brighten the long, weary night,
No love nor peace, nor one ray of light;
No blood-washed soul with face beaming bright,
No loving smile in that region of night;

No mercy, no pity, pardon nor grace,
No water, Oh, God, what a terrible place:
The pangs of the lost no human can tell,
Not one moment's ease — there is no rest in Hell.

Hell, the prisonhouse of despair,
Here are some things that will be there:
Fire and brimstone are there, we know,
For God in His Word hath told us so:
Memory, remorse, suffering and pain,
Weeping and wailing, but all in vain;
Blasphemer, swearer, hater of God,
Christ-rejecter while here on earth trod;
Murderer, gambler, drunkard and liar,
Will have his part in the lake of fire;
The filthy, the vile, the cruel and mean,
What a horrible mob in Hell will be seen:
Yes, more than humans on earth can tell,
Are torments and woes of Eternal Hell.

eX — EXCLUSION

The dictionary gives the meaning of exclusion as "the state of being excluded." Exclude means "to shut out; to put out. Exclude implies keeping out what is already outside." In speaking of the holy city, new Jerusalem, the abode of the saints of God for eternity, God says: "And there shall in no wise enter into it any thing that defileth, neither whatsoever worketh abomination, or maketh a lie: but they which are written in the Lamb's book of life" (Revelation 21:27).

"For without are dogs, and sorcerers, and whoremongers, and murderers, and idolaters, and whosoever loveth and maketh a lie" (Revelation 22:15). Verse 15 makes it clear that the unsaved will be "without" the city, or outside — they cannot enter that beautiful place, but are excluded from it forever.

Someone has written: "Thus they are totally separated from all the things they were fond of in the present world. At the same instant will commence another loss: that of the persons whom they loved. They are torn away from their nearest and dearest relatives; their wives, husbands, parents and children. All the pleasures they ever enjoyed in these, is lost, gone, banished away, for there is no friendship in hell.

"But they will then be sensible of a greater loss than all they have enjoyed on earth. They have lost their place in Abraham's bosom; in the paradise of God. It seems that the Apostle had this in view when he spoke of those 'who shall be punished with everlasting destruction from the presence of the Lord.' Banishment from the presence of the Lord is the very essence of destruction to a spirit that was made for God. And if that banishment lasts forever, it is 'everlasting destruction'." (*The Lost Soul's First Day in Eternity*, pp. 50-51).

Y — YEARNING

Yearn means "to feel mental uneasiness from longing desire; to be filled with eager longing; to desire; to long for; crave." D. M. Fletcher writes in his "Soliloquy of A Lost Soul," the yearning of a soul in Hell:

At last I am in hell. In spite of all my resolutions not to come, I am here to suffer the just demands of a broken law. O God, can it be that I, who was taught the way of truth, virtue and Heaven, should choose sin and eternal damnation?

Death and the judgment are past. The time of repentance has slipped away. Mercy's door is forever shut. I would not heed the warning voice of God, though it thundered in my ear night and day, from my cradle to my grave. I hardened my heart and said I will not yield. At last death came; I tried to repent, but my heart would not melt, and my eyes refused to shed a tear. I passed into eternity a damned soul. The worm that never dies has coiled its slimy folds around my naked heart, and in it fastened its venomous fangs. Merciful God, pity me! But the white-winged angel of mercy has forever flown. The fiends with their bony hands are grasping for my defenseless soul. Away, ye demons, ye shall not touch me. Ah they have me at last; it is useless for me to resist. Is there none to deliver — none great God, none! I turned my back on Thee; now Thou dost refuse to hear my cry of anguish.

The flames of damnation are wrapping my soul in

shrouds of eternal misery. Oh, that I had a drop of water to quench this raging thirst that consumes me: but there is no water here. Demons laugh at my agony, and exultant shout: Enjoy the wages of sin forever! Forever! O God, I have been here but one short hour, and I have suffered more than a thousand tongues can tell and must I forever suffer thus? Through the ceaseless ages yet to come must I still suffer on? None to heed my bitter prayer; none to say it will soon be over? It is forever! Forever!

The darkness is intense; broken only by the lurid flashes of Divine wrath that are thrown like thunderbolts from the hand of a just God! I grope in the darkness to find Him, but plunge over the precipice of despair on the rocks below. Bruised and mangled I rise and stagger on in search of a friend, but not one is found. All are my enemies: I scream for help; and the only help is the echo of my own sad cry and the yells of delight from the throats of demons. Alone! yet multitudes are here; they gnash on me with their teeth, they trample me under their feet. I struggle to rise, and they dash me into the lake of everlasting fire. Alone! Yes, alone! without God, without hope, without Heaven.

Oh, that I had a moment in which to repent; but it will never be given. I sealed my doom. God's mercy was extended; I refused till too late. Now Eternal Justice is being satisfied. 'Tis just. God is love; is just and holy. He is clear, but I am guilty — damned, and that righteously.

An evangelist friend of mine, Chelsea Stockwell, has written a song concerning a person yearning in Hell:

When I was just a little child,
I heard my mother tell
Of Jesus, born in Bethlehem;
I knew it very well.

* * *

I let it go; the years rolled on;
My heart grew harder still,
Now I am lost in hell today
For my own stubborn will.

In Sunday School they taught me of

A Saviour from above
Who traveled all the way to Calvary
Because of His great love.

I neglected then to heed the call.
I said, "I'll let it pass."
But I would give a million worlds
For one more day in class.

One night in a revival, I
Remember very well,
The preacher made it plain,
'Twas either Heaven or Hell.

When they sang, "Almost Persuaded,"
Very near I entered in,
I sold my one last chance to live,
I died, and died in sin.

Lost forever; escaping, no never!
I am lost forever and ever.
I spurned His proferred grace,
I'll never see His face.

The saddest words of tongue or pen,
Are these, "It might have been".

Z — ZERO EXISTENCE

Zero means "figuratively, the lowest point; nothinginess; nullity; a person or thing that has no importance, influence, or independent existence."

In Hell, a person will have "no importance, influence or independent existence." He will be at "the lowest point." W. N. Tidwell has written concerning

Newcomers in Hell

"As we behold this newcomer in Hell, we wonder if he will inquire 'whence this place? What is the origin of it? Why such dark and dismal abode?'

"Then the answer, by some fiend, would be, 'It was prepared for the devil and his angels. It is the penitentiary of the universe.' While prepared for the Devil and his angels all rebels are to be incarcerated here.

"Then I think I hear the newcomer, as he shudders, inquire, 'Where can I find a friend? someone to help me?'

"But the doleful answer comes, 'This is a world where there are no friends. Everyone here hates everybody else. There is no help or mercy here. The world from which you came was a world of mercy but that has all ended now.'

"Then I seemed to hear the friendless soul, as he begins to feel the gnawing worm of a guilty conscience, shriek, 'Then I will end it all. I will commit suicide.'

"But the pitiless answer comes, 'That is impossible here. Back in yonder world men could do that but it is different here. There is no escape from the bitings of a guilty conscience. How it all must be endured I cannot tell, but it must be done. But remember you will never find a friend or helping hand in Hell.'

"But again, I think I hear this newcomer wailing, 'I am so tired, I have had no rest since I left the earth. Please tell me where I may find some place to rest.'

"But, instead of being shown some place of rest, 10,000 fiends with hoarse, stifled voices mutter, 'There is no rest in Hell. As you gaze upon this mighty, restless throng, not one of them has had one moment's rest since they came and the sad part about it all is that, while the countless ages pass by, they can never find rest. This is a world of torment and pain.'

"But another question, 'I have been here sometime now and it has been dark ever since I've been here. I have not seen one ray of light. When will night end and morning come?'

"But again I hear, like the roar of thunder, a chorus of voices as they cry, 'It will always be dark. Morning will never, never come.' Hell is a night without a day. 'No morning will ever dawn on thy gloom.'

"Again he inquires, 'Where can I find some water for I am tormented in this flame. Only a drop. O give me a drop.'

"But again the disappointing answer is given. 'There is no water in Hell. That is a small request but too great to be granted here. The world from which you came was a world of mercy but that day has passed. No favors are granted here.'

"But last of all I hear him wail, 'If there is no light, no

77

love, no friends, no water and no mercy, how long is it to last? How long am I to be here? Surely only a brief time. Pray tell me how long, oh how long?'

"But the response comes ringing through the corridors of the damned, from fallen angels and damned men, it is 'forever and forever.' How it is to be endured we cannot tell you but on the infernal gates, if you have noticed when you entered it read, 'All hope abandon ye who enter here.' On the crest of every fiery billow, and on the grim countenance of every benighted inmate of this dismal world, the word forever seems to be indelibly placed. Your destiny is fixed. Your doom is sealed. Time has passed and eternity, which shall never end, has begun. It is all too late now. Christ died to save you but you refused His mercy and rejected His grace. It is forever and forever too late.

"Too late, too late, to all farewell
My doom is fixed, and I am forced to tell,
As long as God and Heaven shall dwell,
My soul, my soul is lost in Hell."
—From "The Voice of the Nazarene"

Although God says, "for a fire is kindled in mine anger, and shall burn unto the *lowest hell*" (Deuteronomy 32:22), David rejoices in God's salvation and utters these words of praise to God: "For great is thy mercy toward me; and thou hast delivered my soul from the *lowest hell*" (Psalm 86:13). Through repentance toward God and faith toward our Lord Jesus Christ we can be delivered from "zero existence," "the lowest point," and go to Heaven and "be the children of the Highest" (Luke 6:35).

II

WHAT MEN HAVE SAID ABOUT HELL

Men have tried to deny an eternal Hell in their various arguments against it.

Men Who Have Said There Is No Eternal Hell

Some groups say there is no Hell. Dana McClean Greely, in *Life* Magazine, said, "From a Unitarian point of view, there is no heaven or hell. Theologically such an idea is repulsive and unacceptable in the light of the moral affirmation of man." (*Life* Magazine, July 28, 1967, p. 21).

Unity school of Christianity teaches concerning Heaven and Hell: "Both are states of mind, and conditions, which people experience as a direct outworking of their thoughts, beliefs, words, and acts." (*The Metaphysical Bible Dictionary*, p. 271).

Christian Science teaches concerning Hell: "Hell is mortal belief; error, lust . . . suffering and self-destruction, self-imposed agony, effects of sin." (*Science and Health*, 1916, 588:1-3).

Spiritualism, or spiritism, says, "Hell, I may say, drops out altogether, as it has long dropped out of the thoughts of every reasonable man. All spirit people of wisdom know that there is no burning hell, no fearful devil." (*The New Revelation*, 1918, A. Conan Doyle, p. 68). Theosophy's teaching is: "We believe in no hell or paradise as localities." (*Esoteric Christianity*, 1957, p. 212, Vesant).

When all the views concerning the future condition of the unsaved are analyzed and classified they could be stated in three main classes: the annihilation theory, the restoration theory, and the everlasting punishment fact.

The Annihilation Theory

Some people teach that the wicked will be annihilated. The word "annihilate" means *to reduce to nothing, to wipe out of existence*. Two main theories are taught: one, that the wicked will be given a second chance to be saved, and if the second chance to accept Christ is rejected, then the wicked person is put out of existence immediately; the other, that there will be a period of punishment and then annihilation will be experienced.

The teaching that the wicked will be annihilated, also called conditional immortality, has not found acceptance in the Church, but is held largely by the false cults such as Jehovah's Witnesses and Seventh-Day Adventists. Charles T. Russell, the founder of Jehovah's Witnesses, stated, "Life is God's gift, and death (annihilation) is the penalty he prescribes." "The penalty of the second chance for life will be the second death, which is annihilation." (*Studies in the Scriptures*, Vol. 1, pp. 128, 151).

Paul Tillich stated, "Eternity as a quality of the divine life cannot be attributed to a being which as condemned is separated from the divine life. Where the divine love ends, being ends; condemnation can only mean that the creature is left to the non-being it has chosen. The symbol 'eternal death' is more expressive when interpreted as self-exclusion from eternal life and consequently from being." (*Systematic Theology*, II, p. 284).

Those who hold this view reason that death means cessation of existence. There is abundant evidence to prove that this is not so. The rich man in Luke 16:22,23 died, but he did not cease to exist. Death is not cessation of existence but a change in the condition of existence.

False teachers quote Scriptures which apply to the final destiny of the wicked and try to prove that the wicked will be annihilated, using words like "destroy", "destruction", "perish", etc.

It is impossible to make these words mean annihilation. For instance, in Psalm 78:45 we read: "He sent frogs among them [the Egyptians] which *destroyed* them." If the word *destroyed* meant annihilation, the frogs would have put the Egyptians out of existence. Of course, this was not so. Again in Job 19:10, Job complained: "He hath *destroyed* me on every side. . . ." If the word *destroyed* meant annihilation it would mean that Job was put out of existence on every side. In speaking of Christ, the writer of Hebrews said "that through death he might *destroy* him that had the power of death, that is, the devil" (Hebrews 2:14). He surely did not put the devil out of existence. He is very much alive today and will be in existence forever, according to Revelation 20:10. When God says that the wicked "shall be punished with everlasting *destruction* from the presence of the Lord, and from the glory of his power" (II Thessalonians 1:9), He means that the unsaved will be banished from the presence of the Lord and from Heaven forever. The Greek word for *destroy* is *apollumi*, which does not mean to annihilate, but it means "mar", "ruin", or "rendering unfit for the intended use." *Apollumi* is also the Greek word from which the word "perish" is translated. When these words are applied to the wicked, they mean that those who do not believe on the Lord Jesus Christ will be marred, ruined, and unfit for their intended use, and will be separated from God forever and ever.

Herbert W. Armstrong teaches that the wicked will be resurrected at the close of the millennium, then only to be annihilated. (Armstrong, *Lazarus and the Rich Man*, Passadena, Radio Church of God, 1953).

The Seventh-Day Adventists teach: "the finally impenitent, including Satan, the author of sin, will, by the fires of the last day, be reduced to a state of non-existence, becoming as though they had not been, thus purging God's universe of sin and sinners. . . ." (*Seventh-Day Adventists Answer Questions on Doctrine*, p. 13, Washington, D. C., Review and Herald Publishing Association, 1957).

The Restoration Theory

This is a theory that all of the wicked will finally be reconciled to God. It is called by some universalism, the belief that all of God's creation will ultimately be redeemed, including the devil and all of his angels, or demonic spirits. Origen was the first well-known preacher of this doctrine, but at the second Council of Constantinople (A.D. 553) the Church condemned his views, and since then the Christian Church has rejected universalism. Those who advocate this theory believe that punishment is remedial, that God is a God of love and He will neither annihilate the wicked not punish them forever.

Karl Barth taught that all men are elected and redeemed in Jesus Christ and need only to know this (*Church Dogmatics*, IV, 1, 129). Professor C. H. Dodd, a Vice-President of the British and Foreign Bible Society, Chairman of the transalation of the New English Bible, New Testament, also engaged on the New English Bible, Old Testament, said in a book he wrote, *The Bible Today*: "As every human being lies under God's judgment, so every human being is ultimately destined, in His mercy, to eternal life." (p. 118).

Leslie Weatherhead teaches that "the Good Shepherd

at last will bring every soul into the fold, for he himself gave men the picture of the Good Shepherd not content with ninety-nine percent of successes, but seeking the lost sheep 'until he find it'." (*The Christian Agnostic*, pp. 285-86).

The Confession of 1967 of the United Presbyterian Church makes room for universalism, if not actually to endorse it. It speaks of the second coming of Christ, but makes no mention of Hell. It tells of Christ's role as judge but says nothing of eternal retribution as a possible consequence of His verdict.

Emil Brunner says in his book *Eternal Hope*: "God confronts man with the unequivocal demand that he should recognize and endorse the prior decision which God has already made concerning him by electing man to belong to Himself. . . . The doctrine of forgiving Grace — the doctrine of justification — finds its crown in a proclamation of universal redemption." (*Eternal Hope*, London, 1954, pp. 177,178,182).

Rev. Henry E. Jacobs, D.D., writing in *That Unknown Country* summarized: "As certain as eternal life is life without end, just so sure is eternal death death without end. . . . No encouragement whatever can be afforded, by any word of Scripture, for any doctrine either of Restorationism or of annihilationsim." (p. 551).

The Everlasting Punishment Fact

This is the Biblical teaching, as has been shown from the Old Testament, the words of Christ, testimonies of the apostles, and the descriptions of the Bible. P. Schaff said: "Everlasting punishment always was and always will be the orthodox theory." (*History of the Christian Church*, Vol. II, p. 606, Scribners, 1910, New York).

The Greek word *aionios* occurs seventy times in the New Testament. Thayer's New Testament Greek Lexicon gives the meaning of the word *aionios* as "without beginning or end, that which always has been and always will be; without beginning, without end, never to cease, everlasting." The New Standard Dictionary defines *eternal* as "having neither beginning nor end of existence, from everlasting to everlasting; having no end, that will endure forever, everlasting; having no beginning."

In the following word *aionios*, translated "eternal" or "everlasting", is used concerning:

God — Romans 16:26
The King — I Timothy 1:17
The Holy Spirit — Hebrews 9:14
Salvation — Hebrews 5:9
Redemption — Hebrews 9:12
Inheritance — Hebrews 9:15
Glory — II Timothy 2:10; I Peter 5:10
Honor and Power — I Timothy 6:16
Kingdom of Jesus — II Peter 1:11
Life — John 3:16
Weight of glory — II Corinthians 4:17
Things not seen — II Corinthians 4:18
Building of God — II Corinthians 5:1
Gospel — Revelation 14:6
Consolation — II Thessalonians 2:16
Covenant — Hebrews 13:20
Purpose of God — Ephesians 3:11
Habitations — Luke 16:9
Damnation — Mark 3:29
Punishment — Matthew 25:46
Destruction — II Thessalonians 1:9
Judgment — Hebrews 6:2
Fire — Matthew 18:8; 25:41; Jude 7

The same word *aionios* which describes God, the Holy Spirit, etc., also describes the duration of fire, damnation, punishment, destruction, and judgment. C. H. Mackintosh logically asks: "What warrant has anyone, be he ever so learned, to single out seven instances from the seventy in which the Greek word 'aionios' is used, and say that in those seven it does not mean everlasting, but that in all the rest it does? None whatever." (*Elemental Theology*, p. 317).

The same word describes the life of the righteous per-

son and the punishment of the unrighteous person in
Matthew 25:46: "And these shall go away into everlast-
ing punishment: but the righteous into life eternal."
"Everlasting" and "eternal" are both translated from the
Greek word *aionios*.

The Greek phrase "unto the ages of the ages" (once
"unto the age of the age," Hebrews 1:8), occurs twenty-
two times in the New Testament, fourteen of these times
in the book of The Revelation. It is translated "for ever
and ever" twenty-one times and "for ever more" once:

To God be glory — Galatians 1:5; Philippians 4:20
To God be honour and glory — I Timothy 1:17
To the Lord Jesus Christ be glory — II Timothy 4:18;
    Hebrews 13:21
To the Throne of Christ — Hebrews 1:8
To Jesus Christ be praise and dominion — I Peter 4:11
To God be glory and dominion — I Peter 5:11
Jesus is alive — Revelation 1:18
God lives — Revelation 4:9, 10; 5:14; 10:6; 15:7
Unto God and Christ be blessing, and honour, and glory,
    and power — Revelation 5:13
Unto God be blessing, glory, wisdom, thanksgiving,
    honour power, and might — Revelation 7:12
Christ shall reign — Revelation 11:15
The righteous shall reign — Revelation 22:5
Smoke of the torment of the wicked — Revelation 14:11;
    19:3
Devil, beast, and false prophet tormented — Revelation
    20:10

You will notice that this phrase is used ten times in
reference to the duration of glory, honor, praise,
dominion, blessing, and power of God and of Christ; once
of the throne of Christ; once of the reign of Christ; six
times concerning the duration of the life of God and of
Christ; and three times concerning the duration of the
punishment of the wicked. There is no doubt about the
endlessness of the first nineteen references. There
should not be any doubt about the last three.

Richard DeHaan, in his booklet, "The Eternal Fire,"
concluded four messages on Hell with these words: "We
repeat our conviction that the lost will spend eternity in

conscious existence under punishment in Hell. The Word of God gives us a solid basis for this belief; in fact, it leaves us with no alternative. The expressions, 'fire unquenchable' (Matthew 3:11), 'that never shall be quenched' (Mark 9:43,45), the worm that 'dieth not' (Mark 9:44,46,48), along with the use of 'everlasting' and 'forever', most assuredly denote that this punishment will be eternal." (pp. 30-31).

William Elbert Munsey, in his book *Eternal Retribution* spoke of the Saviour's sermons: "The blessed Saviour sat down probably on the eastern horn of the Hattin, a ridge between Tabor and Tiberias, and preached His first sermon. . . .

"This was His first sermon; now hear His last — 'Woe unto you, scribes and Pharisees, hypocrites . . . Woe unto you, ye blind guides . . . ye fools and blind . . . Woe unto you scribes . . . Woe unto you thou blind Pharisee . . . ye serpents, ye generation of vipers, how can ye escape the damnation of hell?'

"Cursings and blessings go together — Love incarnate can curse a sinner, Love incarnate can damn a sinner, and if Love incarnate can curse and damn a sinner it can do it for all eternity.

"O Eternity! let thy ages triumph, thy cycles roll, but thou canst not crumble or scar the walls of Hell, or rust and break its locks or silver the hair of God, who has sworn by His eternal self that the sinner shall die. The pendulum of thy horologe over the gates of woe vibrates through all aeons, and says 'forever, and ever' — 'forever, and ever' — 'forever, forever and ever' — its sounding bells striking off the centuries, the ages — the cycles. The appalling monotony of its pendulum — going — going — going — repeating still, 'forever, and ever' — 'forever, and ever' — 'forever, and ever' — O Eternity! God has wound up thy clock and it will never run down — and its tickings and beatings are heard by all the lost — 'forever, and ever' — 'forever, and ever' — 'forever, and ever.' God being my judge I would die to save you this day." (pp. 90-91).

Men Who Have Said There Is An Eternal Hell

The following quotations are from men of the first century to the present day. I'm listing them in alphabetical order, not in chronological order. These men are all in agreement that there is an eternal Hell awaiting lost sinners.

NEHEMIAH ADAMS: "The Scriptures reveal a future state of reward and punishment. They teach that the body and soul will be joined in future happiness and misery. Christ teaches that God can destroy both body and soul in Hell. Future punishment will therefore be a natural operation of moral laws, sustained and made effectual by the hand of God upon the sinner, who, by his state of depravity, will be made susceptible to misery forever. The essential elements of misery remain in the wicked after death. Redemption by Christ is represented as having for its object salvation from final perdition. No passage in the Bible discloses the future repentance of the wicked. The Bible closes with an express declaration of the future unchangeableness of character." (*Scriptural Arguments for and Reasonableness of Future Endless Punishment*, pp. 102-103).

HYMAN J. APPLEMAN: "Should you make your abode in hell, you will see the burning faces, the glazed eyes, the tortured hands of fellow prisoners of damnation. You will recognize, God forbid, husband, wife, father, mother, brother, sister, son, daughter, friend, neighbor, that you could as easily have taken to heaven as dragged down to hell. Oh, that awful mass of weeping, wailing humanity that inhabits hell! They, too, cry one heaven-searching cry to God, but, alas, too late. All cry that endless refrain, 'Forever! Forever! Forever!' Beyond God forever! Beyond Christ forever! Beyond the Spirit forever! Beyond the Bible forever! Beyond the Gospel forever! Beyond the cross forever! Beyond the blood forever! Beyond tears forever! Beyond repentance forever! Beyond faith forever! Beyond confession forever! Beyond time forever! Beyond eternity forever! Forever! Forever! Forever!" (*Hell — What Is It?* pp. 19-20).

ARMINIAN BAPTISTS IN ENGLAND: These Baptists affirmed belief in "an eternal judgment . . . which is unalterable and irrevocable." (W. J. McGlothlin, *Baptist Confessions of Faith*, Philadelphia, American Baptist Publication Society, 1911, p. 103).

AUGSBURG CONFESSION OF 1530: "Christ shall appear to judge . . . ungodly men and the devils shall He condemn unto endless torment." (P. Schaff, *Creeds of Christendom*, New York, Harper Brothers, 1881, Vol. III, p. 17).

EMERY H. BANCROFT: "We know the enormity only by God's own declaration with regard to it, and by the sacrifice which He has made to redeem us from it. As committed against an infinite God, and as having in itself infinite possibilities of evil, it may itself be infinite, and may deserve infinite punishment. Hell, as well as the cross, indicates God's estimate of sin." (*Christian Theology*, p. 369).

RICHARD BAXTER: "What a subtle tempter Satan is. What a deceitful thing sin is. What a foolish creature corrupted man is. A subtle tempter indeed, who can persuade the greatest part of the world to go willfully into everlasting fire, when they have so many warnings and dissuasives as they have. A deceitful thing is sin indeed, that can bewitch so many thousands to part with everlasting life, for a thing so base and utterly unworthy! A foolish creature is man indeed, who will be so cheated of his salvation for nothing, yea, for a known nothing; and that by an enemy and a known enemy. You would think it impossible that any man in his wits should be persuaded for a trifle to cast himself into the fire, or water, or into a cold pit, to the destruction of his life. And yet men will be enticed to cast themselves into hell." (*A Call to the Unconverted*, p. 119).

HENRY WARD BEECHER: "I do not accept the doctrine of Hell because I delight in it. I would cast in doubts if I could, till I had filled Hell up to the brim. I would destroy all faith in it, but that would do me no good; I could not destroy the thing. I cannot alter the stern fact. The exposition of future punishment in God's Word is not to be regarded as a threat, but as a merciful declaration. If in the ocean of life over which we are bounded for eternity, there are rocks and shoals, it is no cruelty to chart them down, it is an eminent and gracious mercy." (*Ready for Anything*, pp. 78-79).

BELGIC CONFESSION (1561): "The consideration of the judgment is justly terrible and dreadful to the wicked and ungodly . . . who shall be convicted by the testimony of their own consciences, and being immortal, shall be tormented in that everlasting fire which is prepared for the devil and his angels." (P. Schaff, *Creeds of Christendom*, Vol. III, p. 433).

JOE BOYD: "Now the physical side of this world is temporary, but Hell's fire is eternal. The rich man in the account given by Jesus was tormented in the 'flame' (Luke 16:24). The pitiful part about it is that he is still there in the same flame.

"You say, 'But, Brother Joe, the flame will burn out, or it will consume the body.' Friend, have you never read of the fire in the burning bush that did not consume the bush? God can make an eternal fire and can give the sinners a body that will not be consumed. God can do anything but contradict Himself. He can never go back on His Word. He is unchangeable. He has said that these shall go away into everlasting fire, and His Word cannot be changed." (*The Sword of the Lord*, Friday, November 13, 1970, p. 6).

FRED BROWN: "Some object to the preaching of this truth [Hell] on the grounds that children shouldn't hear it. It shocks them, according to some. I was shocked by it when I was seven. So shocked to learn that I was a sinner and on my way to hell, that I ran straight into the arms of Christ. God knows better than man, what to put in His Word, and all that is in the Word should be preached to all ages." (*The Biblical Faith of Baptists*, Book 3, p. 211).

HARRY BUIS: "We have been led to a serious study of this subject [Hell] for several reasons. One is that there is no other doctrine that is clearly taught in Scripture which is so generally denied or ignored in our modern theological world. . . .

"But more serious than the wide-spread denial of the doctrine is the attitude of many evangelicals toward it. Many dare not preach it; while others go to the opposite extreme, describing hell in such gross and lurid terms that they often do more harm than good. . . .

"Another reason for our writing on the subject is that the man on the street fails to take this doctrine seriously, as is shown by his constant use of the word 'hell' in a thoughtless and meaningless way. . . .

"For these reasons, we write on the subject of hell, with the earnest prayer that our work on the subject may be used of God in keeping some precious souls from experiencing hell's terrible reality." (*The Doctrine of Eternal Punishment*, pp. IX-XII).

JOHN CALVIN: John Calvin refers to Hell as "this gulf of perdition" and declares that "no description can equal the severity of the Divine vengeance on the reprobate, their anguish and torment are figuratively represented under corporal images; as darkness, weeping, and gnashing of teeth, unextinguishable fire, a worm incessantly gnawing the heart." (John Calvin, *Institutes of the Christian Religion*, Book iii. Translation by J. Allen, 7th Edition, Vol. II, p. 264).

B. H. CARROLL: He warned stubborn unbelievers: "You are just as certain for Hell as if you were there today." (R. G. Lee, *Bread from Bellevue Oven*, p. 58).

LEWIS SPERRY CHAFER: "The conclusion of the

matter is that God, because of His holiness, cannot save the lost unless His holy demands are met for the sinner, as they are met in the death of Christ; and to be unsaved or outside the grace of God as it is in Christ, is to be destined to eternal retribution. God can do no more than to provide a perfect salvation, which is provided at infinite cost. When love would pay such a price that a sinner may be saved and holiness remain untarnished, it ill becomes finite men to tamper with these immutable realities. Those who resent the idea of eternal retribution are, in fact, resenting divine holiness." (*Systematic Theology*, Vol. IV, p. 433).

F. W. CONRAD: "From the facts and arguments just presented, the conclusion is inevitable, that the testimony of the conscience of every rational and responsible being in the moral universe, on earth, in heaven, and in hell, corroborates the testimony of the perfect conscience of God, that the eternal damnation of the wicked is just." (*That Unknown Country*, p. 204).

A. C. DIXON: "When the wicked, in the flashlight of the Judgment Day, shall see themselves and their sins as they are, they will accept everlasting punishment as just retribution. Their sense of justice will approve it. It would appear to them an incongruous thing for God to take them to Heaven; as incongruous, indeed, as it would appear to a guilty impenitent criminal if the king of England, instead of sending him to prison, as he deserves, should take him into the palace as an associate for his wife and children.

"A cemetery is a necessity. The bodies of the dead must not be left in the homes of the living. A little child died in the family of a former parishioned; the poor mother, crazed with grief, would not consent to its burial. She stood, like Rizpah, over its little lifeless form and would not allow undertaker or husband to touch it. After a week of such heart-rending experience, the husband was compelled to remove her by force to another room, while some friends went with the little form to the cemetery. To have kept the dead with the living would have been unkindness to the living and have done the dead no good. And thus every cemetery is an argument for Hell. The spirit of the dead soul is like a dead body in that it is in a state of moral putrefaction and carries with it the deadly contagion of sin. If it refuses to receive life, it must of necessity be placed apart with its spiritually dead companions." (R. G. Lee, *Bread from Bellevue Oven*, pp. 56-57).

W. E. DOWELL: "There is a day of judgment! God must and will punish sin! Man will give an account unto God, and man will pay the final penalty for his sin, summed up in the words of Revelation 20:15, 'And whosoever was not found written in the book of life was cast into the lake of fire.' This is the second death. That is not an imaginary hell. It is a real hell. It is not imaginary fire and brimstone. It is a real fire and brimstone, and souls and bodies that cannot perish, but are capable of the greatest amount of suffering, will be plunged into hell and suffer; not for a day, nor week, nor a month, nor year, nor a century, nor a millennium, but for all the ceaseless ages of eternity! What a price for lost souls to pay!" (*The Biblical Faith of Baptists*, p. 178).

JONATHAN EDWARDS: "Consider the fearful danger you are in! It is a great furnace of wrath, a wide and bottomless pit, full of the fire of wrath, that you are held over in the hand of that God whose wrath is provoked and incensed as much against you as against many of the damned in Hell. You hang by a slender thread with the flames of divine wrath flashing about it, and ready every moment to singe it and burn it asunder; and you have no interest in any Mediator, and nothing to lay hold of to save yourself, nothing to keep off the flames of wrath, nothing of your own, nothing that you've ever done, nothing that you can do, to induce God to spare you one moment.

"Therefore, let everyone that is out of Christ now awake and flee from the wrath to come. The wrath of Almighty God is now undoubtedly hanging over every unregenerate sinner." (*Sinners in the Hands of An Angry God*, Booklet, pp. 21,34).

ENGLISH BAPTISTS: ". . . the unsanctified, which have not known God, and have not obeyed the Gospel of Jesus Christ, shall go into everlasting fire." (W. J. McGlothlin, *Baptist Confessions of Faith*, pp. 64-65).

C. H. FOWLER: "It remains for us to call attention to the fearful fact that the Bible declares that the punishment of the wicked or finally impenitent is eternal. The wicked depart into everlasting fire. The smoke of their torment ascendeth up for ever and ever. They shall weep and wail and gnash their teeth. They have no rest day nor night. The door is shut and the wicked are ordered to depart. . . .

"Surely, one can find no hope of escape through these terms. *The doctrine of eternal punishment must be true.*" (*That Unknown Country*, pp. 320-21).

W. H. FRENCH: "We cannot determine what shall be the future of the wicked or of the righteous by the principles of natural law or by anything in the material world. It is a doctrine to be learned of the Word of God, and the teachings of that Word are always in accord with sound reason and true logic. . . . To ignorance, the picture of hell is revolting, but enlightened reason assents to the Word of God in all that it teaches respecting it and in all that it is declared to be. . . .

"That the Word teaches future punishment is evident from the common understanding of it by all classes of Christians. The Jews so understood the teaching of the Old Testament; they believed it taught future retribution, and the Saviour when in the world neither corrected this impression nor taught contrary to it, but, on the contrary, warned them of it. . . . And it is true today, that the Scriptures are understood by the masses of the readers of them, as teaching the doctrine of the punishment of the wicked after death. . . .

"Blessed be God for His Son Jesus Christ, Who came into the world to save souls from such death." (*That Unknown Country*, pp. 327,332,338).

GERMAN BAPTISTS: They declared their belief in a world-judgment in which God would "pronounce on all the godless the judgment of eternal damnation." (W. J. McGlothlin, *Baptist Confessions of Faith*, p. 353).

F. W. GRANT: "It may suit you, alas, to soften down the terrors of the day of wrath, but what if you *should* find God is just in inflicting severer judgment than your conscience, or your want of it, now allows as righteous? Oh, ponder these words of the very One who came to save! 'Everlasting fire,' 'undying worm,' are after all realities. They *abide*, the solemn figures of judgment to come. On the other hand, God's grace invites you — His compassionate appeal is, 'Come now, and let us reason together, saith the Lord: though your sins be as scarlet, they shall be as white as snow . . . but if ye refuse and rebel, ye shall be devoured with a sword; for the wrath of the Lord hath spoken it' (Isaiah 1:18-20), and Christ says, 'Him that cometh to me, I will in no wise cast out' (John 6:37)." (*Man and the Future State*, pp. 237-38).

OLIVER B. GREENE: "I have heard men and women boast that they were not afraid of hell. They were sure they could endure the torment and therefore they would 'take their chances.' To such people I would offer a challenge: Put just one finger over the flame of one little match and hold it there in the flame until the match burns out! There is no person alive who would voluntarily do such a thing — nor could anyone endure the pain even if he (or she) would be willing to. The pain from even so small a flame would be so excruciating it would force withdrawal long before the match extinguished itself. In comparison with that, think of the rolling flames of the inferno of hell, flames that will never cease to burn, and the spirits of the wicked will be tormented on in those flames day and night forever and ever." (*Hell,* pp. 71-72).

HEIDELBERG CATECHISM (1563): "His (God's) justice requires that sin, which is committed against the most high majesty of God, be also punished with extreme, that is with everlasting punishment of body and soul." (P. Schaff, *Creeds of Christendom,* Vol. III, p. 311).

HERSCHEL H. HOBBS: "Many people deny the existence of hell. Yet Jesus said more about hell than He did about heaven. Such denial is due more to wishful thinking and sentimental reasoning than to an interpretation of the factual teaching of the Bible. To say that a merciful God would not make a hell is to examine only one facet of God's nature. He is love. But He is holiness and righteousness also. God sends no one to hell. Each person goes there of his own will despite all that God in Christ has done to prevent it." (*What Baptists Believe,* pp. 116-17, Broadman Press, Nashville, 1964).

CHARLES HODGE: "The common doctrine is, that the conscious existence of the soul after the death of the body is unending; that there is no repentance or reformation in the future world; that those who depart this life unreconciled with God, remain forever in this state of alienation, and are, therefore, forever sinful and miserable. This is the doctrine of the whole Christian church, of the Greeks, of the Latins, and of all the great historical protestant bodies." (*Systematic Thelogy,* p. 869, Scribner, 1888, iii, New York).

JOHN HOLLIDAY: "Without a profound recognition of the certainty of judgment and reality of hell, no sinner can know the serious implications of rejecting the Gospel, no Christian can grasp the full significance of his salvation, no preacher can fulfill his high mission, no Sunday School teacher is adequately equipped for his task, no parent can discharge his sacred trusteeship, no Baptist church is prepared to carry out Christ's great commission, and no Baptist Congress, were it ten thousand times bigger than this impressive assembly, could hope to bring to our generation the awakening that is so desperately needed." (*The Biblical Faith of Baptists*, p. 142).

J. W. HOTT: "The doom of the wicked, in suffering and punishment, after death is eternal. . . .

"So far as we can see, the punishment of unpardoned sin against the love, mercy, and offer of salvation from God, must be eternal, because there is infinite demerit in this sin. It is a disregard of infinite and eternal obligation. The safety of the moral universe demands the punishment of the wicked. Without it, anarchy would overthrow the throne of God, and turn the moral universe into chaos. . . . It is held that the Bible teaches the endless punishment of the wicked in the same language, respecting its duration, in which it teaches the eternal happiness of the righteous, and that this is presented in the strongest words expressing the idea of eternal, or endless, duration, in use in the languages in which the Bible is given to man, 'these shall go away into everlasting punishment; but the righteous into life eternal'." (*That Unknown Country*, pp. 502-503).

JACK HYLES: "How about putting your finger in the fire and saying, 'One second,' — pull it out?

"No, you wouldn't do it. Yet my friends, Hell is longer than one second! Hell is longer than two seconds! Hell is longer than five seconds! Hell is longer than ten seconds! Hell is longer than ten minutes! Hell is longer than ten days! Hell is longer than ten weeks! Hell is longer than ten months! Hell is longer than ten years! Hell is longer than ten thousand years! Hell is longer than ten million years! Hell is longer than ten billion years! Hell is longer than ten trillion years! There are many people who would not be so foolish as for one single second to put their finger in the fire of a kitchen stove, yet who are plunging their souls toward a place of torment where they will burn for millions and billions of years forever, without hope in the world to come! Oh, think of it! Hell is eternal. It never ceases. The duration of Hell!" (*The Sword of the Lord*, p. 10, July 8, 1960).

IRENAEUS: He affirmed his belief in the return of Christ "that He may execute righteous judgment over all: sending into eternal fire the spiritual powers of wickedness, and the angels who transgressed and apostacized, and the godless and lawless and blasphemers among men." (P. Schaff, *Creeds of Christendom*, Vol. II, p. 14).

HARRY IRONSIDE: "And what about the rich man in Luke 16:19-31? He also died and was buried, and we follow his disembodied spirit into the other world. Jesus said, 'In hell he lifted up his eyes, being in torment.' Now, my friends, there have been times when I would have taken that out of the Bible if I could, and even tonight I can well understand the feelings of Richard Baxter as he prayed, 'Oh, for a full heaven and an empty hell!' I have searched this Book, and read scores of volumes penned by theologians of all shades of opinion, to try and find one ray of hope for men who died in their sins, but I have never been able to find it. . . .
"Accept the testimony of this Book, receive the Saviour it reveals, or go into the outer darkness forever! There is no other alternative. It must be Christ or hell and to reject the one is to choose the other." (*Death and Afterwards*, pp. 28,30).

SAM JONES: "I believe in a bottomless Hell; and I believe that the wicked shall be turned into Hell. The legitimate end of a sinful life is Hell." (R. G. Lee, *Bread from Bellevue Oven*, p. 57).

ROBERT W. LANDIS: After writing over 500 pages in his book *The Immortality of the Soul*, concludes: "My soul rests with delight ineffable upon the expiatory power of my Saviour's blood, and there alone rests all my hopes for eternity. I own from my inmost soul the perfect justice of the sentence which would consign me as a sinner to an eternal severance from God and salvation, and I neither know, nor can I imagine any way by which to escape that sentence, except the mercy proffered through our Lord Jesus Christ, to Whom be praise and glory and dominion forever and ever.

"This same deliverance is freely proffered to you, and, wherever you may be, you are as much in need of it as I am. You too have entered upon an existence from which there is no escape, and your probationary state will soon be past forever. If you die in a state of sin and alienation from God, there is no hope for you. . . . you can now escape if, without delay, you will truly accept the mercy offered through the redemption that is in Christ Jesus. He is waiting to be gracious to you; hear then His voice, and harden not your heart." (*The Immortality of the Soul*, p. 508).

R. G. LEE: "Some say: 'I hate Hell.' So do I. But if a man is going to be a preacher of Christianity, he should preach the doctrines of Christianity. I hate to think of anybody going there. But nobody can hate Hell out of existence. I hate snakes, but my hatred does not exterminate them. I hate rats, but rats still live. If we're Christians, we hate sham, but sham is here. If we walk as wise people and not as fools, we hate the works of the flesh. But adultery, fornication, lasciviousness, idolatry, witchcraft, hatred, variance, emulations, wrath, strife, seditions, heresies, envyings, murders, drunkenness, revellings, and such like are with us. We all should hate lying, but lying is here. We hate dishonesty, but dishonesty is abroad. I hate infidelity, but infidelity is here. I hate liquor, but liquor is here. If hate were an exterminator, I could get rid of sin by midnight. Disbelief in Hell does not put out its fires. Disbelief in poison does not do away with the deadliness of poison. You might believe you could play with nitroglycerine without danger, but that belief will not keep men from picking up your fragments in a basket. Disbelief and unbelief do not alter facts. THERE IS A HELL!" (*Bread from Bellevue Oven,* p. 52).

HERBERT LOCKYER: "It is mercilessly clear that there is a hell, and that the wicked are to be turned into it. Not to preach it is to smooth the way to perdition for lost souls. If men were walking hard by the edge of a precipice, would we not be branded as murderers if we did not cry out loud to warn them? Dare we silently stand by while souls tramp the road to eternal torment? The idea of such terrible woe may be abhorrent to many, but our course is clear. We must warn sinners that finally to reject Christ means that they must endure the consequences of their sin and become the objects of divine wrath." (*Is There A Hell?* p. 31).

DANIEL ALBRIGHT LONG: "Founded in ethics, in law, and in judicial reason, as well as taught by the Author of Christianity, it was the prevailing opinion in the Early Church that the punishment of the impenitent would be endless." (*That Unknown Country,* p. 613).

MARTIN LUTHER: "So God, at the day of judgment, will separate all things through fire, the righteous from the ungodly. The Christians and righteous shall ascend upward into heaven, and there live everlastingly, but the wicked and ungodly, as the dross and filth, shall remain in hell, and there be damned." (H. T Kerr, *A Compend of Luther's Theology,* p. 238, Westminister Press, 1943, Philadelphia).

R. S. MacARTHUR: "The New Testament uncovers hell. Men have known but little of this fearful abyss, but for the teachings of the loving Lord Himself. As the cross most fully displays the love of God, so the teaching of Him Who died upon the cross most fully reveals the wrath of God against all unrighteousness. Never was preaching so characterized by what men have called the 'hell-fire' element, as was the preaching of the Son of God. He uttered the most fearful woes that came from human lips; but these most terrible woes were baptized in tears of infinite love." (*That Unknown Country*, p. 665).

CLARENCE EDWARD MACARTNEY: "Eternal punishment is an inescapable inference from the plan of salvation. God is the author of eternal salvation . . . Eternal life and happiness are granted to those who are saved by faith in Christ. He died for sinners. He gave His life a ransom for many. Men who believe and are saved have life eternal. The plain inference from all this is that if there is a heaven, there must be a hell; and if there is eternal life through faith in Jesus Christ, there must be eternal death without Christ. In short, if men are saved, there must be some real fate from which they are saved." (*Putting on Immortality*, pp. 154-55).

ROBERT MURRAY M'CHEYNE: In his last message before he died, preached on the afternoon of March 12, 1843, in St. Peter's, he said: "Brethren, there is a hell. It was God's plan that there should be vessels of wrath as well as vessels of mercy. . . . O do not dream! All will not be saved."

T. C. McCROSSAN: "Columbus Green once asked Theodore Parker, the very best Unitarian Greek scholar in America, this question: 'As a Greek scholar, and not as a Theologian, will you please tell me what the Scriptures really teach regarding the final condition of the finally impenitent?' Dr. Parker replied, 'There is no doubt that Jesus taught the endless suffering of the wicked, but I do not accept the doctrine on His authority.' And why? Because he did not believe that Christ was really God, and, therefore, being only a man, He might have made a mistake.

"Now Dr. Parker's conclusion, as we will prove, must be the conclusion of every real Greek scholar. When you find any man, claiming to be a Greek scholar, who denies that Christ taught a Hell and eternal punishment, you will know for a certainty that he is deceiving you." (*The Bible: Its Hell and Its Ages*, p. 36).

GEORGE MacDONALD: "There are only two kinds of people in the end: those who say to God, 'Thy will be done,' and those to whom God says, in the end, 'Thy will be done.' All that are in Hell, choose it. Without this self-choice there could be no Hell. No soul that seriously and constantly desires joy will ever miss it." (C. S. Lewis, *The Great Divorce*, p. 69, The Macmillan Company, New York, 1946).

TOM MALONE: "I certainly stand in awe and marvel when it comes to the matter of hell. It is such an awful fact. Men ought to face it. I pray, God, that it may dawn upon your heart today that there is a hell to which sinners go. I am not merely concerned in this message with impressing the fact of hell upon the hearts and minds of the unsaved. But the Christian people across America and around the world need to be constantly reminded that hell is no myth. Hell is no fable. Hell is an awful reality, as taught by the Lord Jesus Christ in the entire Word of God." (*The Baptist Vision*, December 15, 1956, p. 1).

J. R. MANTEY: "Thus we see that the New Testament teaches that in addition to physical death there is also for the unsaved a spiritual death which is identified as the second death and constitutes the eternal penalty for having ignored God and the Lord Jesus Christ. 'This is the second death, even the lake of fire'." (*Bibliotheca Sacra*, Vol. 112, No. 448, October, 1955, p. 343).

JIM MERCER: "The old preachers were right. It is better to be Hell-scared than Hell-scarred.

"I am a Hell-scared Christian. I went to bed many a night thinking I would wake up in Hell. I knew I deserved to go to Hell for my sins. I tell you it is great relief to know Christ in the forgiveness of sins! It is a wonderful difference and it can be your experience if only you open your heart to the Saviour." (*The Sword of the Lord*, September 6, 1957).

ADOLPHE MONOD: "I did everything I could to avoid seeing eternal suffering in the Word of God, but I did not succeed in it . . . When I heard Jesus Christ declare that the wicked would go away into eternal punishment and the righteous into eternal life, and that therefore the sufferings of the one class would be eternal in the same sense that the felicity of the other would be, . . . I gave in; I bowed my head; I put my hand over my mouth; and I made myself believe in eternal suffering." (*Premiere Serie de Sermons*, p. 391).

D. L. MOODY: "Some people come to me and say: 'You do not really believe there is such a thing as everlasting retribution and future punishment, do you?' Yes, I do. The same Christ who talked to us about that bright upper world has given us a picture of the lost. In this portion of Scripture, [Luke 16:19-31] it has been drawn very vividly by the Master Himself. We hear a voice coming up out of the lost world — of the man that was once upon the earth — and fared sumptuously every day, and yet was lost, not for time, but for eternity. Over and over again, Christ warned those who hung upon His words. Once, in speaking to His disciples, He spoke about the worm that dieth not; about one being cast into Hell, where the worm dieth not." (*The Sword of the Lord*, December 12, 1969).

HENRY MORRIS: "Outside the city, and undoubtedly far outside the new earth itself, but somewhere in the universe, will be the lake of fire, prepared for the devil and his angels (Matthew 25:41), but serving also as the eternal prison of all who must be judged according to their works (Revelation 20:12-15). . . .
"The flames of the fiery lake will burn without light, as hell is to be a place of utter darkness (Jude 13; II Peter 2:17). The awful environment will sear the soul as well as the body (Matthew 20:28), in the midst of unending corruption and sin (James 3:6; Revelation 22:11). Every least token of the love and grace and power of God will be

forever removed as its inhabitants are to be 'punished with everlasting destruction from the presence of the Lord, and from the glory of his power' (II Thessalonians 1:9). All who have preferred to be independent of God, walking in their own ways and neglecting His great salvation, will thus eternally be granted that freedom from God which they desire. They must be removed from the earth, since it will be thenceforth where God will dwell (Revelation 21:3), and transported to some far-distant body of flaming darkness, forever." (*Bibliotheca Sacra*, October, 1968, pp. 298-99).

WILLIAM ELBERT MUNSEY: In speaking of the lost soul he says: "See it — yonder — yonder — yonder — yonder. It goes that way: **LOST! LOST!** *lost!*. It comes this way shrieking lost! *lost!* **LOST!** till our hearts stand still with horror. Scream on, fly on, cursed and ruined spirit: no battlemented walls of towering jasper will ever meet thy gaze, or furnish a resting place for thy weary pinion. Fly on, lost soul, forever, no angel of mercy will ever cross thy solitary way, or overtake thee in thy wanderings. Lost spirits! blackened with the curse of thy God, fly on, and repeat in despairing cry at the chorus of thine own horrible death-march, '*lost, lost,*' where no echoes will ever mock thy misery. Immortal soul! lost in boundless, bottomless, infinite darkness, fly on, thou shalt never find company till the ghost of eternity will greet you over the grave of God, and thou shalt never find rest till thou art able to fold thy wings on the gravestone of thy Maker.

"And the Judge will say to the angels: 'Bind him hand and foot, and take him away, and cast him into outer darkness; there shall be weeping and gnashing of teeth' (Matthew 22:13)." (*Eternal Retribution*, pp. 103-104).

NEW HAMPSHIRE CONFESSION OF 1830: ". . . that the wicked will be adjudged to endless punishment, and the righteous to endless joy; that this judgment will fix forever the final state of men in heaven or hell on principles of righteousness." (W. J. McGlothlin, *Baptist Confessions of Faith*, p. 307).

WILLIAM W. ORR: "Hell will be terror, without one mitigating feature. Pain, without the slightest chance of alleviation, will be unbearable. The flaming torment will be so severe that one will beg piteously for a drop of water to cool his tongue. Suffering of the body will be so terrible that the sinner will grind his teeth in agony. Coupled with this will be anguish of spirit in the realization that Hell could have been avoided. Conscience will stab and nag and accuse forever. Perhaps the doomed sinner will recall the day he rejected the call of the Spirit for the last time." (*The Tragedy of Hell and How to Escape It*, p. 24).

IAN PAISLEY: "Tonight we are coming to an authority that cannot be challenged. We are coming tonight to a Book that stands amidst the ruin of empires and the decaying of the worlds — the blessed Book of God. If I accept this Book, then, friend, I accept unreservedly that there is a Hell. Fifty-six times, in the plainest, most unmistakable, stupenduous, and overwhelming way, this Bible declares there is a Hell! God has not said it once; if this Book declared it but once, we would and must accept it. God has not said it twice, God has not said it three times, but God has said fifty-six times in this Book that there is a place of punishment for impenitent souls, that men unconverted, unredeemed, unsaved shall go to Hell! That's what the Book says. If I'm going to accept the Bible, then I'm going to accept the doctrine of Hell. It stands upon the foundation of the Word of God." (*The Sword of the Lord*, November 28, 1969, p. 10).

ARTHUR W. PINK: "The final portion of the wicked is described as 'the blackness of darkness forever' (Jude 13). Unrelieved will be their fearful sufferings; interminable their torments. No means of escape. No possibility of a reprieve. No hope of deliverance. Not one will be found who is able to befriend them and intercede with God for them. They had the offer of a Mediator often made them in this world; but no such offer will be made them in the Lake of Fire. 'There is *no peace*, saith my God to the wicked.' There will be no resting-place in Hell; no secret corner where they can find a little respite; no cooling fountain at which they may refresh themselves. There will be no change or variation of their lot. Day and night, forever and ever, shall they be punished. With no prospect of any improvement they will sink down into blank despair." (*Eternal Punishment*, p. 28).

JOHN R. RICE: "The Bible repeatedly, from one end to the other, teaches that Hell is a place of fire. The modernists and liberalists teach that there is no Hell. Many who claim to be fundamentalists or conservatives say that the Bible passages teaching a physical Hell with literal fire are figurative in meaning. This is, I believe, because they have not studied the matter afresh for themselves in the Bible, but have simply accepted the current teachings without seeing for themselves what God has said. But it has resulted that the whole Christian world has lost its fear of Hell, and with it has lost the soul-winning passion. To Christians all over the world, Hell has cooled. That means that Calvary means less, there is less emphasis on redemption by the blood of Christ, there is less teaching about sin, very little warning of judgment, and almost universal powerlessness and fruitlessness on the part of Christians. Our hearts are turning toward modernism while our heads still accept the letter of the Bible. At the same time, the unbelieving world tends more and more to scoffing and scorn about the things of God.

"Thus it seems necessary for Christians to make a renewed study of the Bible doctrine of Hell. Oh, if there is a literal Hell of eternal torment, if it has real fire in it, and if poor lost souls will suffer eternally in physical torment as well as mental torment in this physical Hell of literal fire, then we ought to know it!

"With this in mind, I call your attention to what seems

to me to be the overwhlming proof that Hell is a literal lake of fire, a place of literal, physical torment for the unconverted, the Christ rejecter who dies without being born again.

"There is abundant proof in the Bible that Hell is a literal, physical place." (*Twelve Tremendous Themes,* pp. 172-73).

LEE ROBERSON: "Every man who is not under the blood of Jesus Christ is lost. Your child is lost and Hell-bound if your child has come to the age of accountability and has not accepted Christ. The dearest loved one you have is lost and condemned forever without Jesus Christ. Your relatives and your friends who are not in Christ will be lost in the fires of Hell forever if they should suddenly die.

"Lost friend, if your life should suddenly cease, Hell would be your eternal portion. If tonight you should step outside of this auditorium and be struck by a passing car, you would be in eternal Hell, lost forever." (*Death . . . and After?,* p. 87).

J. C. RYLE: "Let others hold their peace about Hell if they will: I dare not do so. I see it plainly in Scripture, and I must speak of it. I fear that thousands are on that broad road that leads to it, and I would fain arouse them to a sense of the peril before them.

"What would you say of the man who saw his neighbor's house in danger of being burned down, and never raised the cry of 'fire'? Call it bad taste, if you like, to speak of Hell. Call it charity to make things pleasant and speak smoothly, and soothe men with the constant lullaby of peace. From such notions of taste and charity may I ever be delivered! My notion of charity is to warn men plainly of their danger. My notion of taste is to declare all the council of God. If I never spoke of Hell, I should think I had kept back something that was profitable, and should look on myself as an accomplice of the Devil.

"Beware of new and strange doctrines about Hell and the eternity of punishment. Beware of manufacturing a God of your own — a God who is all love, but not holy — a God who has a Heaven for everybody, but a Hell for none — a God who can allow good and bad to be side by side in time, but will make no distinction between good and bad in eternity. Such a God is an idol of your own, as really as Jupiter or the monstrous image of Jugernaut, as true an idol as was ever molded out of brass or clay. The hands of your own fancy and sentimentality have made him. He is not the God of the Bible; and besides the God of the Bible there is no God at all. Your heaven would be no heaven at all. A heaven containing all sorts of characters mixed together indiscriminately would be miserable discord indeed. Alas for the eternity of such a heaven! There would be little difference between it and Hell. Ah reader, there is a Hell! Take heed lest you find it out too late." (*The Sword of the Lord*, August 28, 1970, p. 1).

L. R. SCARBOROUGH: "The Word of God is very clear both in the Old Testament and in the New in the fact that there are two destinies for the souls of men. There is a Heaven revealed in God's Word. There is a hell clearly told of in the Divine Book. There are two hundred sixty-four chapters, I think, in the New Testament. In two hundred thirty-four times, nearly one verse for every chapter in the New Testament, alone, God says that there is a place of eternal punishment. If life's road twenty-six miles long had on it two hundred thirty-four sign boards saying, 'This road leads to hell' I think I would go another road. There is a great deal more said in the Bible about the place of eternal punishment than there is about heaven. I wish to say tonight that I believe the doctrine of eternal punishment stands or falls with the diety of Christ. If you say that there is no hell, then you say that the Bible is unreliable; and if the Bible is unreliable then Jesus Christ is not the Son of God and we are in a hopeless world without any anchor for the soul." (*Prepare to Meet God*, p. 30).

J. A. SEISS: "Ho, ye unbelieving men, — ye dishonest men, — ye profane men, — ye lewd men and women, — ye slaves of lust and appetite, — ye scoffers at the truth of God, — 'How can you escape the damnation of Hell?' (Matt. 23:33). Ye men of business, — ye whose souls are absorbed with the pursuit of gain, — ye people of wealth without riches toward God, — ye passengers on the voyage of life, without prayer, without church relations, without concern for your immortal good, your God, or the eternity before you, — hear: 'Hell hath enlarged herself, and opened her mouth without measure, and your glory, and your multitude, and your pomp, and your rejoicing shall descend into it!' (Is. 5:14). Ye almost Christians, lingering these many years on the margin of the King-dom, looking in through the gates, but never quite ready to enter them, intending but never performing, often wishing but still postponing, hoping but without right to hope, — the appeal is to you: 'How shall ye escape if ye neglect so great salvation?' (Heb. 2:2-4). And ye who call yourselves Christians but have forgotten your covenant promises, — ye Terahs and Lot's wives, who have started out of the place of sin and death, but hesitate halfway, and stay to look back, — ye baptized Elymases, and Judases, and Balaams, who, through covetousness and feigned words make merchandise of the grace of God, — see ye not that 'your judgment now of a long time linger-eth not, and your damnation slumbereth not!' (2 Pet. 2:3.) And if there be any one oblivious or indifferent toward these great matters, — asleep amidst the dashing waves of coming retribution, — the message is to you: 'What meanest thou, O sleeper? Arise, call upon thy God, if so be that God shall think upon thee, that thou perish not!' (Jon. 1:6) For if any one be not found written in the Book of Life, he must be swallowed up by the Lake of Fire." (*The Apocalypse*, pp. 481-82).

WILLIAM G. T. SHEDD: "The strongest support of the doctrine of Endless Punishment is the teaching of Christ, the Redeemer of man. . . . The mere perusal of

Christ's words when he was upon earth, without note or comment upon them, will convince the unprejudiced that the Redeemer of sinners knew and believed that for impenitent men and devils there is an endless punishment." (*The Doctrine of Endless Punishment*, Scribner's, 1887, p. 12).

HAROLD B. SIGHTLER: "Modernists and false religions have perverted the Word as to remove the fact of Hell. Many sinners scoff at the preaching of Hell. They turn aside any warning of judgment, they think the idea of Hell has passed away with the last generation. Sixty seconds after death they shall find out the truth of the Word; there is fire in Hell." (*The Sword of the Lord*, July 24, 1959, p. 5).

OSWALD J. SMITH: "Now God has an asylum. He, too, knows that the saved and the unsaved could never be happy together, and so in His asylum —, which, by the way, was never prepared for man — the insane will one day have to be put. . . .

"God's asylum is called Gehenna, and it is mentioned twelve times in New Testament Scriptures; eleven times by Christ Himself and once by James. John calls it the Lake of Fire and the Second Death. I have called it the Madhouse of the Universe.

"This asylum is a place of conscious suffering. Such words as fire, weeping, wailing, the gnashing of teeth are used to describe it. People do not weep when they are happy, nor do they wail unless they are miserable. When they gnash their teeth they must be suffering real pain.

"So terrible is it that Jesus recommended the loss of hand, foot and eye in preference to being consigned to it." (*The Message of Hope*).

PAUL SMITH: "This is Hell — everlasting death — a dying, with all of its agony, that goes on forever. How else can I describe it? How can I picture the pain, the weeping, the wailing, the gnashing of teeth? There is no pain on earth great enough to be compared with the pains of

Hell. Napoleon, a man who was supposed to have the hardest of hearts, one day rode across the battlefield. As he rode, his horse stepped on a poor, wounded man, just about to die, and in his dying breath the wretched soldier rose up and gasped. Whereupon Napoleon cried out in horror, 'Oh God, what pains a man may suffer!'

"Could you and I put our ear to the entrance of the world of spirits for a moment and listen to the cries of the damned, we too would turn back with countenance blanched and cry, 'Oh God, what pains a man may suffer!'

"Could all the misery that has ever horrified the staffs of our hospitals be gathered together, it would not convey the least conception of the pains of those who are doomed to dwell in eternal fire and everlasting burning. Body, mind, and spirit — all will be tormented; each one racked on a bed of fire; every fibre strained to its utmost; every nerve made a highway for the searing feet of pain. Even Jesus Christ, the most compassionate of all preachers, preached the most awful Hell. He called it a place 'where their worm dieth not, and the fire is not quenched' (Mark 9:48)." (*The Sword of the Lord*, November 23, 1956).

C. H. SPURGEON: "But, in Hell there is no hope. They have not even the hope of dying — the hope of being annihiliated. They are forever — forever — forever — lost! On every chain in Hell, there is written 'forever.' In the fires there blazes out the word 'forever.' Up above their heads they read 'forever.' Their eyes are galled, and their hearts are pained with the thought that it is 'forever.' Oh! if I could tell you tonight that Hell would one day be burned out, and that those who were lost might be saved, there would be jubilee in Hell at the very thought of it, but it cannot be — it is 'forever' they are 'cast into utter darkness'." (*Ready for Anything*, p. 80).

W. C. STEVENS: "The message of a real and literal hell, definitely localized and materialized, is the Spirit's implement in a fearless, faithful preacher's mouth, for bringing sinners out of carelessness and practical un-belief into a needed terrifying realization of the danger before them." (*Revelation, the Crown-Jewel of Biblical Prophecy*).

LEHMAN STRAUSS: "Let not one of us be misled by the teaching that the fires of Hell mean the torments of conscience. The consciences of most individuals never seem to be bothered by their treatment of Jesus Christ. But God will see to it that the unrighteous do not remain in the present hades in a disembodied state, but will be raised to receive resurrection bodies and to spend eternity in Hell fire." (*An Examination of the Doctrine of Jehovah's Witnesses*, pp. 43-44).

BILLY SUNDAY: "I wish I could believe that there is no Hell. Nothing would rejoice or delight me more, when I leave here, than to know that every man, woman and child in Pittsburgh had repented and accepted Jesus Christ as their Saviour. But if men persist in living in sin, if they persist in rejecting Jesus Christ and defying God, then it is right and proper that there should be a Hell in which they be confined. If men choose sin rather than salvation, if they choose iniquity rather than God, then it is right and just — it is for the good of the universe and for the glory of God that there be a Hell." (*The Sword of the Lord*, March 8, 1968, p. 1).

T. DeWITT TALMADGE: "I will simply state that God, fifty-six times in the plainest, most unmistakable, stupendous, and overwhelming way, declares that there is a hell. It is burning now. It has been burning a long while. Yes, I will go further, and say that there is a possibilty that some reader of these words may spend eternity in the lost world. Nothing but the hand of an outraged, defied, insulted, long-suffering, indignant, omnipotent God keeps any of us this moment from sliding into it. . . .

"I believe there is a hell. If I had not been afraid of hell, I do not think I should have started for heaven." (*That*

Unknown Country, pp. 876-77).

WILLIAM J. R. TAYLOR: "But this doctrine of the endless retributions of eternity does account clearly, positively, and satisfactorily for all the teachings of the Bible on the subject, and for all the facts of human consciousness and experience in relation to it. Were it not so clearly revealed in the Holy Scriptures of the Old and the New Testaments, no believer in God would accept it. I agree with the living preacher whose heart is as tender as his faith is strong, in his saying, 'Nothing but the fear of God, nothing but the hand of God upon me, could ever drive me to preach the doctrine of endless hell-fire. Hell is balanced by heaven. That speaks whole volumes. We have nothing to do with hell but to escape it. Our business is to seek and reach heaven'." (*That Unknown Country*, pp. 891-92).

TERTULLIAN: He declared that Christ "will come again in glory to take the saints into the enjoyment of life eternal . . . and to condemn the impious to everlasting fire, both parties being raised from the dead and having their flesh restored." (J. N. Kelly, *Early Christian Creeds*, London, Longman's, 1960, p. 85).

CAM THOMPSON: "It is certain that I would now be in Hell, if I had not had by me a copy of the Word of God. As it is impossible to find hope in the Word of God for those who have gone into the fires eternal, so it is impossible to find hope in the Word of God for those who have never heard. Men are born lost, in a world that is lost, of a race that is poisoned to its core with sin. Who can misunderstand the meaning of this verse: 'He that believeth on the Son, hath everlasting life: and he that believeth not the Son shall not see life, but the wrath of God abideth on Him' (John 3:36)." ("The Awful Reality of Hell", A Tract).

R. A. TORREY: "Men, I have hunted my Bible through for one ray of hope for men that die impenitent, just a ray of hope that can be called such when the passage is properly interpreted by the right laws of exegesis, and I have failed after years of search to find one. I am familiar with the passages men quote, but they will not bear the burden placed upon them when carefully interpreted in their context with an honest attempt to discover what they really mean, and not to make them fit a theory. The New Testament does not hold out one ray of hope for men and women that die without Christ. Anyone who does, dares to do what God has not done. 'For ever and ever' is a never-ceasing wail of that restless sea of fire. Such is hell, a place of bodily anguish, a place of agony of conscience, a place of insatiable torment and desire, a place of evil companionship, a place of shame, a place without hope." (*Real Salvation*, p. 55).

L. T. TOWNSEND: "The Bible clearly shows that God's threatenings against the sinner are not confined to this life, but extend over into the life to come, and that the punishments there to be inflicted may properly be termed *hell torments*. . . .

"The Scriptures, interpreted as we interpret other literature, leave no room for doubt that God utters threats, not only against impenitent sinners in this life, and also in the life to come, but likewise threatens to punish finally impenitent sinners time and world without end." (*Lost Forever*, pp. 104-105, 116-117).

JACK VAN IMPE: "Seventy percent of the ministers polled recently said, 'We do not believe in a hell.' Well, I don't care if everyone doesn't believe in it. I have a Bible that says 162 times in the New Testament that there *is* such a place, and I believe God." (Sermon, "Hell Without Hell").

G. BEAUCHAMP VICK: "I believe the Bible. When God says 'fire,' He means fire. When He says 'Hell,' I think He means Hell. When He speaks of everlasting punishment, I believe He means just exactly that. There *is* a Hell. The Bible says so and all laws of logic demand it. Our only source of information concerning Hell is in the Bible, the Word of God. No one who has experienced the torments of Hell has ever come back to tell us, for, 'There is a great gulf fixed'." (Sermon, "What the Bible Says About Hell").

TOM WALLACE: "Some have asked why preach on the horrible subject of Hell? I preach on Hell because I know that some of you who listen to the sermon or read these lines will spend eternity there. It is my duty to warn you to flee the wrath to come.

"Hell is a terrible subject and the thought of burning flesh brings chills to me. Nothing is more painful nor carries a more nauseating odor than burned flesh. I was visiting in our local hospital not long ago and I stepped into a room where a man was on his knees with his head down on his folded arms on the bed. I walked up to the man and said, 'Sir, are you praying?' He answered, 'No, preacher, my back is burned so bad that this is the only position that I can get any relief.' For several days I went there to see him and every time he was on his knees. I was reminded that in Hell relief won't come on the knees." (*The Sword of the Lord*, August 9, 1963, p. 8).

ISAAC WATTS: "O could we but perceive a thousandth part of the horror that is contained in an eternal hell, an eternal banishment from the face and favour of God, and the eternal impressions of His anger, we should never give ourselves rest one moment, till we had returned to God by a sincere repentance, and were reconciled to Him that made us; till we fled for refuge to the blood of Jesus, and to His sanctifying grace, which is the only hope that is set before us. We should never give ourselves leave to lie down, or awake in quiet while we were destitute of a saving interest in the salvation of Christ, and had attained to some clear evidence of it, and a well-grounded hope." (*The End of Time*, p. 325).

JOHN WESLEY: "Put your finger in the candle. Can you bear it for one minute? How then will you bear to have your whole body plunged into a lake of fire burning with brimstone?" (*Ready for Anything*, p. 78).

WESTMINSTER CONFESSION (1647): "God hath appointed a day wherein He will judge the world in righteousness . . . the wicked who know not God, and obey not the Gospel of Jesus Christ, shall be cast into eternal torments, and be punished with everlasting destruction from the presence of the Lord and from the glory of His power." (P. Schaff, *Creeds of Christendom*, Vol. III, p. 671).

LESLIE H. WOODSON: "The only conclusion at which we can arrive in view of the limited study to which we have exposed ourselves in this book is that there is a hell. *It is clearly taught in the Bible. . . . No man is so good that he can escape hell on his own merits. And no man is so bad that he has no chance.* Men are not destined to hell because of their sins but solely because they do not accept Christ as Saviour and Lord. Not all men will be saved but all could be *if they would only receive the Son of God by faith.*" (*Hell and Salvation*, p. 107).

KENNETH S. WUEST: This Greek scholar who made a thorough study of the duration of future punishment, after quoting a number of Greek scholars such as Moulton and Milligan, Cremer, Thayer, Liddell and Scott, to prove his point, concluded with these words: "Thus, God's Word clearly teaches that the sufferings of the lost will be unending." (*Wuest's Word Studies in the Greek New Testament*, Vol. 3, *Treasures from the Greek New Testament*, p. 43).

I have quoted almost a hundred men — authors, Confessions of denominations, doctors of divinity, educators, evangelists, pastors, presidents of Christian schools and seminaries, recognized scholars, and others — from the first century to our own day, and could easily have quoted from others. As Dr. Robert G. Lee stated: "These are only a few flowers from the garden of truth — only a few voices amidst many voices of truth — giving attestations concerning Hell." (*Bread from Bellevue Oven,* p. 58).

Yes, there is an eternal Hell — the Old Testament says there is; Christ says there is; the apostles say there is; the New Testament says there is; men of God through the centuries say there is. Now I want to tell how people can keep out of it.

III

WHAT TO DO TO
KEEP OUT OF HELL

A famous artist painted a picture showing a beautiful forest, a lovely wooded area. But his teacher said, "Never paint a forest without painting a path leading out." In the preceeding chapters I have painted a picture of Hell — what the Bible says about it; what the Old Testament said about it; what Jesus said about it; what the apostles said about it; and what men have said about it. I now want to paint a path leading out. Thank God, we don't have to go there.

Years ago, the noted missionary Adoniram Judson spent many days giving out Gospel tracts on the borders of Siam and China. Two or three months later a letter came to him from one of the distant fields. It read as follows:

"Sir, we hear there is an eternal hell. We are afraid of it. Do give us a writing that tells us how to escape it."

117

I pray that many readers of this book will be like this man as he spoke of Hell — "afraid of it." I realize there are many people who boast of not being afraid of Hell. One man declared openly, "I am seventy years of age, and have never seen such a place as Hell, after all that has been said about it." His little grandson, about seven years of age, who had heard his grandfather make this statement, asked him, "Granddaddy, have you ever been dead yet?" Then the conversation ended. People who die unsaved will immediately see Hell because they go there as soon as they die (Luke 16:22-23).

I agree with evangelist Jim Mercer when he said, "It is better to be Hell-scared than Hell-scarred." The Bible says, "The fear of the Lord is the beginning of knowledge: but fools despise wisdom and instruction" (Proverbs 1:7), and "The fear of the Lord is the beginning of wisdom" (Proverbs 9:10).

Jesus Christ warned, "But I will forewarn you whom ye shall fear: Fear him, which after he hath killed hath power to cast into hell; yea, I say unto you, Fear him" (Luke 12:5). God is the One Who has power to cast people into Hell after death and a wise person will fear Him and prepare for eternity.

Over an eighteen-year period the Prairie Bible Institute in Canada asked the incoming students to give the motive, as far as they knew, as to why they became a Christian. Out of 2,507 students during those years:

65% said they were moved through the motive of fear.
6% said they were moved through the motive of love.
(Other motives given were the desire for peace, joy, satisfaction; some did not know the motive.)

Over ten times more of these students were saved through the motive of the fear of God and judgment and Hell than were saved through the motive of the love of God.

Rev. T. DeWitt Talmadge stated: "I believe there is a hell. If I had not been afraid of hell, I do not think I should have started for heaven."

I heard an evangelist in Michigan tell about his conversion to Christ. He said that as a young lad he heard his father preach a message on Hell and according to him, "It scared me to life." Usually people speak of being "scared to death," but this young fellow was "scared to life" — eternal life, through putting his trust in Jesus Christ, Who gives everlasting life to all those who receive Him (John 10:27-29). A true fear of Hell has sent many a soul to Heaven.

Jesus Christ spoke very pointedly to some people in His day: "Ye serpents, ye generation of vipers, how can ye escape the damnation of hell?" (Matthew 23:33). I want to answer that question in this last chapter, and help anyone who is like the man who wrote to Judson concerning Hell: "We are afraid of it. Do give us a writing that tells us how to escape it."

Rene Pache wrote: "To be lost, man need do nothing; he is a sinner, condemned by the law of God; and he need simply stay as he is to go directly to hell." (*The Future Life*, pp. 323-24). It does not require a decision to go to Hell.

G. Summer Wemp has written a four-page tract with the words, "What to Do to Go to Hell?" on the front cover. As you open the tract, the inside two pages are blank. On the last page he says, "Surprised? We need to do nothing to go to Hell because we have already done it. We all stand as guilty sinners before God, we deserve to be punished (Ezekiel 18:4)." Then he continues to tell the reader that he can be saved through receiving Jesus Christ as personal Saviour and tells him that if he does that, "you won't go to Hell either.'

God does not want people to go to Hell. In Ezekiel, God told the prophet: "Say unto them, As I live, saith the Lord God, I have no pleasure in the death of the wicked; but that the wicked turn from his way and live: turn ye, turn ye from your evil ways; for why will ye die, O house of Israel?" (Ezekiel 33:11). Spurgeon said, "Turn in time, or burn in eternity." In I Timothy 2:3-4 we are told: "For this is good and acceptable in the sight of God our Saviour; Who will have all men to be saved, and to come unto the knowledge of the truth." In these verses we see that God takes no pleasure in the death of the wicked, but commands them to turn from their sins and live and He desires all men to be saved. The rich man in Hell knew that if his five brothers repented they would not go to Hell (Luke 16:30).

REPENTANCE

Jesus made it clear that if people did not repent they would perish, or go to Hell: "except ye repent, ye shall all likewise perish" (Luke 13:5). He gave the reason for His coming into the world: "I came not to call the righteous, but sinners to repentance" (Luke 5:32).

There are those today who say that repentance is not necessary, that it was only for the Jews. One writer made this statement: "Repentance is Jewish. Jews could repent because they were in covenant relationship with God and had violated that covenant. But Gentiles had never known such a relationship. They are dead sinners, therefore they cannot repent until after they are born of God." This is definitely not true, because when Peter preached to the Gentiles in the house of Cornelius, as recorded in Acts 10, the result of that preaching was that those who heard him were saved, and it was said concerning them: "That hath God also to the Gentiles granted repentance unto life" (Acts 11:18).

Professed preachers of grace say that to preach repentance invalidates the grace of God; consequently there are millions of people who have joined our churches in America (about 132,000,000 Americans are church members), who have given mental assent to the Gospel, who have never repented of their sins. Men like D. L. Moody, R. A. Torrey, Robert G. Lee, and others estimate that ninety percent of the church members of America are lost. No person can be saved until he believes on the Lord Jesus Christ, and no one can believe on the Lord Jesus Christ until he truly repents. Jesus commanded, "repent ye, and believe the gospel" (Mark 1:15).

Peter speaks of repentance: "The Lord is not slack concerning his promise, as some men count slackness; but is long suffering to usward, not willing that any should perish, but that all should come to repentance" (II Peter 3:9).

Paul told the people at Athens: "And the times of this ignorance God winked at; but now commandeth all men everywhere to repent" (Acts 17:30). He spoke to King Agrippa and related what he did after Jesus Christ commissioned him to preach: "I was not disobedient to the heavenly vision: But showed first unto them at Damascus, and at Jerusalem, and throughout all the coasts of Judea, and then to the Gentiles, that they should repent and turn to God, and do works meet for repentance" (Acts 26:19-20). He called for the elders of the church at Ephesus and told them: "I kept back nothing that was profitable unto you, but have showed you, and have taught you publickly, and from house to house, Testifying both to the Jews, and also to the Greeks, repentance toward God, and faith toward our Lord Jesus Christ" (Acts 20:20-21).

In order to escape the damnation of Hell, God's Word is plain:

A person must repent.

A person must believe on the Lord Jesus Christ.

The word "repentance" in the New Testament is *metanoia* in the Greek, and it means "to change the mind," or "to have another mind," and it involves both a turning from sin and a turning to God. It touches the intellect, the emotions, and will. Repentance is not reformation, not contrition, not penance, but it is a change of mind which will lead to a change of action. It is possible to have a change of action and not have a change of mind.

Repentance is a change of mind about sin, self, God, and Jesus Christ. Charles C. Ryrie said of repentance: "If repentance is understood to mean changing your mind about your sin, being sorry for your sin, this will not necessarily save. . . . People can be sorry for their sin without wanting to accept the forgiveness of a Saviour.

"But if repentance means changing your mind about the particular sin of rejecting Christ, then that kind of repentance saves, and of course it is the same as faith in Christ. . . . That kind of repentance saves, and everyone who is saved has repented in that sense." (*A Survey of Bible Doctrine*, p. 139).

Lewis Sperry Chafer stated, "Therefore it is dogmatically stated as language can declare, that repentance is essential to salvation, and that none can be saved apart from repentance, but it is included in believing and could not be separated from it." He continues, "No individual can turn to Christ from some other confidence without a change of mind, and that, it should be noted, is all the repentance a spiritually dead individual can ever effect. That change of mind is the work of the Spirit (Ephesians 2:8)." (*Systematic Theology*, Vol. 3, pp. 373-374).

R. A. Torrey said, "Nothing is so calculated to impress sinful man with a hatred of sin, and abhorrence of self as a sinner, as a real view of God. If then we wish to bring men to repentance, let us bring them face to face with God. This can be effected by showing them God as revealed in His Word. But it must be done in the power of the Holy Spirit." (*What the Bible Teaches*, p. 361).

I do desire in this chapter to "bring men to repentance . . . showing them God as revealed in His Word . . . in the power of the Holy Spirit."

Many people reject the truth of Hell because they say a God of love would never send a person to a place of punishment forever. They say, "I can't believe that a loving God would allow His creatures to suffer forever in a literal Hell." People talk and think like this because they have a faulty concept of God — they think of His love but do not realize that God is also holy and He must punish sin.

The holiness of God is clearly taught throughout the entire Bible. To say that God is holy means that He is absolutely pure and free from all sin and defilement. Here are some verses which speak of the holiness of God.

"Therefore hearken unto me, ye men of understanding: far be it from God, that he should do wickedness; and from the Almighty, that he should commit iniquity" (Job 34:10).

"And one cried unto another, and said, Holy, holy, holy, is the LORD of hosts: the whole earth is full of his glory" (Isaiah 6:3).

"For thus saith the high and lofty One that inhabiteth eternity, whose name is Holy; I dwell in the high and holy place, with him also that is of a contrite and humble spirit, to revive the spirit of the humble, and to revive the heart of the contrite ones" (Isaiah 57:15).

"This then is the message which we have heard of him, and declare unto you, that God is light, and in him is no darkness at all" (I John 1:5).

The holiness of God manifests itself in a hatred of sin. "For all that do such things, and all that do unrighteously, are an abomination unto the LORD thy God" (Deuteronomy 25:16).

"The foolish shall not stand in thy sight: thou hatest all workers of iniquity" (Psalm 5:5).

"God judgeth the righteous, and God is angry with the wicked every day" (Psalm 7:11).

"For the froward is abomination to the LORD: but his secret is with the righteous" (Proverbs 3:32).

"The way of the wicked is an abomination unto the LORD: but he loveth him that followeth after righteousness. The thoughts of the wicked are an abomination to the LORD: but the words of the pure are pleasant words" (Proverbs 15:9,16).

His holiness manifests itself in the punishment of the sinner. "For thou art not a God that hath pleasure in wickedness: neither shall evil dwell with thee. The foolish shall not stand in thy sight: thou hatest all workers of iniquity. Thou shalt destroy them that speak leasing: the LORD will abhor the bloody and deceitful man" (Psalm 5:4-6).

God is holy, He hates sin, and He must punish sin. He is righteous and just and must insist that when a person does not meet His perfect requirements he is to be punished. God has established moral laws based upon His holy nature, and has provided for penalties when these laws are broken. God would be untrue to Himself if He did not administer punishment to those who sin.

Dr. M. R. DeHaan in his booklet *The Lake of Fire*, wrote concerning why God must punish sin:

> The fact of hell rests upon the very foundation of a moral universe. Do away with the punishment of evildoers, and the whole moral fabric and integrity of society breaks down completely.
>
> The basis of all good government is justice. Evildoers must be punished. We have laws to punish the thief, the murderer, the liar, the robber, the traitor, the rebel. No one denies that this is just and right. Every jail and prison in the world is a monument to the necessity of a moral government and the justice of punishing the criminal. What a world this would be if there were no laws to govern, and no penalty for the criminal and transgressor. We even inflict the death penalty for the criminal and the transgressor. We even inflict the death penalty for certain crimes and no one questions the right of the government to do so. Why then object to the right of a sovereign God of heaven and earth to punish His rebelling subjects and creatures? Deny this, and I repeat, the whole moral fabric of the universe immediately breaks down.
>
> This world is so full of inequalities, there must be a reckoning someday. If death ends all, and there is no retribution for evil, how then do we explain the despots who live in luxury here below, oppressing their fellowmen, murdering, pillaging, subjecting others to their atrocities. Think of the Hamans, the Neros, and the Hitlers whose hands are stained with the blood of thousands and millions of innocents. Did death end all for these

men? Is there no punishment for such? Then my faith in the moral integrity of the God of the universe must go by the board entirely. Ah, no, my friend, a God of love who would let sin go unpunished would be no God at all. He would do less than even human justice demands. (*The Lake of Fire*, pp. 11-12).

God's holiness is manifested at the cross, when He sent His only begotten Son, the Lord Jesus Christ, to pay the penalty of sin for us. How hateful sin must be to God for Him to punish it to the utmost deserts in the person of His own Son. We read of the provision of God for our sins in these verses:

"But he was wounded for our transgressions, he was bruised for our iniquities: the chastisement of our peace was upon him; and with his stripes we are healed. All we like sheep have gone astray; we have turned every one to his own way; and the LORD hath laid on him the iniquity of us all" (Isaiah 53:5,6).

"For God so loved the world, that he gave his only begotten Son, that whosoever believeth in him should not perish, but have everlasting life" (John 3:16).

"He that spared not his own Son, but delivered him up for us all, how shall he not with him also freely give us all things?" (Romans 8:32).

"For Christ also hath once suffered for sins, the just for the unjust, that he might bring us to God, being put to death in the flesh, but quickened by the Spirit" (I Peter 3:18).

Stephen Charnock made this tremendous statement: "Not all the vials of judgment that have or shall be poured out upon the wicked world, nor the flaming furnace of a sinner's conscience, nor the irreversible sentence pronounced against the rebellious demons, nor the groans of the damned creatures, give such a demonstration of God's hatred of sin, as the wrath of God let loose upon His Son. Never did Divine holiness appear more beautiful and lovely than at the time our Saviour's countenance was most marred in the midst of His dying groans. This He Himself acknowledges in Psalm 22. When God had turned His smiling face from Him, and thrust His sharp knife into His heart, which forced that terrible cry from Him, 'My God, My God, why hast Thou forsaken Me?' He adores this perfection — 'Thou are holy,' v. 3." (*The Attributes of God*, pp. 45-46).

God has often forgiven sinners, but sin must always be punished — and the sinner is only forgiven because Jesus Christ has borne his punishment. Lewis Sperry Chafer spoke of the holiness of God:"

> "Let it be restated that, if God could save one soul from sin by mere generosity, He could save all souls from sin by generosity and the death of Christ thus becomes the greatest possible divine blunder. It is the fact of unyielding divine holiness which demands either the retribution of the sinner of the death of Christ in his room and stead. God is love, and that love is demonstrated by the gift of the Son that men might be saved; but love and mercy did not circumvent the demand of holiness to save the sinner: They paid its every demand. The conclusion of the matter is that God, because of His holiness, cannot save the lost unless His holy demands are met for the sinner, as they are met in the death of Christ; and to be unsaved, or outside the grace of God as it is in Christ, is to be destined to eternal retribution. God can do no more than to provide a perfect salvation, which is provided at infinite cost. When love will pay such a price that a sinner may be saved and holiness remain untarnished, it ill becomes finite men to tamper with these immutable realities. Those who resent the idea of eternal retribution are, in fact, resenting divine holiness. However, the message of God's grace to sinful men is not merely a proclamation of eternal condemnation; it is rather that the chief of sinners may be saved through the Saviour that infinite love has provided." (*Systematic Theology*, Vol. 4, p. 433).

All of us have sinned and come short of the glory of God (Romans 3:23) and the best we can do in ourselves is spoken of in Isaiah 64:6: "But we are all as an unclean thing, and all our righteousnesses are as filthy rags; and we all do fade as a leaf; and our iniquities, like the wind, have taken us away."

Thank God, that which God's holiness demanded, His grace has provided in Jesus Christ our Saviour and Lord. "He [God] made Him [Jesus Christ] who knew no sin to be sin on our behalf, that we might become the righteousness of God in Him" (II Corinthians 5:21, *New American Standard Bible*).

Every one who repents and believes on the Lord Jesus Christ is accepted by God, forgiven by God, and will never go to Hell.

FAITH

In order to escape the damnation of Hell a person must repent and he must believe on the Lord Jesus Christ. I have spoken of repentance; now I want to say a few words about faith — believing on the Lord Jesus Christ.

Emery H. Bancroft, in his book, *Elemental Theology*, stated, "Faith is the positive aspect of true conversion, the human side of regeneration. In repentance, the sinner turns away from sin, while in faith he turns to Christ. These are inseparable, the one from the other. True repentance cannot exist apart from faith, nor faith, from repentance." (*Elemental Theology*, p. 205).

The New Testament has many references which teach that people are saved by faith in the Lord Jesus Christ, or by believing on Christ. Dr. Lewis Sperry Chafer said concerning this: "Upwards of 115 New Testament passages condition salvation on *believing*, and fully thirty-five passages condition salvation on *faith*, which latter word in this use of it is an exact synonym of the former." (*Systematic Theology*, III, p. 376).

Here are some of those references concerning believing and faith:

"But as many as received him, to them gave he power to become the sons of God, even to them that believe on his name" (John 1:12).

"And as Moses lifted up the serpent in the wilderness, even so must the Son of man be lifted up: That whoso-

127

ever believeth in him should not perish, but have eternal life. For God so loved the world, that he gave his only begotten Son, that whosoever believeth in him should not perish, but have everlasting life. He that believeth on him is not condemned: but he that believeth not is condemned already, because he hath not believed in the name of the only begotten Son of God. He that believeth on the Son hath everlasting life: and he that believeth not the Son shall not see life: but the wrath of God abideth on him" (John 3:14-16,18,36).

"Verily, verily, I say unto you, He that heareth my word, and believeth on him that sent me, hath everlasting life, and shall not come into condemnation; but is passed from death unto life" (John 5:24).

"And this is the will of him that sent me, that every one which seeth the Son, and believeth on him, may have everlasting life: and I will raise him up at the last day. Verily, verily, I say unto you, He that believeth on me hath everlasting life" (John 6:40,47).

"To him give all the prophets witness, that through his name whosoever believeth in him shall receive remission of sins" (Acts 10:43).

"And by him all that believe are justified from all things, from which ye could not be justified by the law of Moses" (Acts 13:39).

"And brought them out, and said, Sirs, what must I do to be saved? And they said, Believe on the Lord Jesus Christ, and thou shalt be saved, and thy house" (Acts 16:30,31).

"For I am not ashamed of the gospel of Christ: for it is the power of God unto salvation to every one that believeth; to the Jew first, and also to the Greek" (Romans 1:16).

"Therefore being justified by faith, we have peace with God through our Lord Jesus Christ" (Romans 5:1).

"That if thou shalt confess with thy mouth the Lord Jesus, and shalt believe in thine heart that God hath raised him from the dead, thou shalt be saved. For with the heart man believeth unto righteousness; and with the mouth confession is made unto salvation" (Romans 10:9,10).

"For by grace are ye saved through faith; and that not of yourselves: it is the gift of God: Not of works, lest any man should boast" (Ephesians 2:8,9).

There is a faith spoken of in the Bible as dead faith: "Even so faith, if it hath not works, is dead, being alone. But wilt thou know, O vain man, that faith without works is dead? For as the body without the spirit is dead, so faith without works is dead also" (James 2:17,20,26). In this same chapter of James God says: "Thou believest that there is one God; thou doest well: the devils also believe, and tremble" (James 2:19). It is not enough to say we have faith, or to believe in God. Saving faith is believing with the heart, which means the whole being: the intellect, the emotions, and will. The faith by which a sinner is saved means to trust Christ, receive Him, rely upon Him, throw the entire weight upon Him. It means to feel your need of Him, to believe that He is able and willing to save you now, and to cast yourself unreservedly upon Him.

Dr. Will H. Houghton, who was president of the Moody Bible Institute when I was a student there, used an excellent illustration of

What It Means to Believe on Christ

When the late Dr. John G. Paton was a missionary in the New Hebrides, he wanted to translate the Gospel of John into the native tongue. He had worked on the Gospel and found that there wasn't a word — at least he couldn't locate a word — in the native tongue which meant "believe." How could he translate the Gospel of John without a word for "believe"? If it is the key word (and it is) and if it is true that the word occurs more than ninety times (and it does), how could you translate it if you didn't have any word to correspond with it? So he laid his manuscript aside.

But one day one of the native workers who had been out over the hills in some Christian service came in to Dr.

Paton's office, and sitting in one chair and putting his feet up on another, he used a native word which meant, "I am resting my whole weight on these two chairs." There was one native word which meant all this — "I am resting my whole weight upon." And Dr. Paton said, "I have my word." He translated the Gospel of John, and every time he needed a word for "believe," he put in the word which meant, "I am resting my whole weight upon."

Let us try it and see how it works. "For God so loved the world that he gave his only begotten Son, that whosoever *resteth his whole weight upon him* should not perish, but have everlasting life" (John 3:16). "But as many as received him, to them gave he power to become the sons of God, even to them that *rest their whole weight upon him*" (John 1:12). Is that it? Yes, that is it! "What must I do to be saved?" "*Rest your whole weight upon* the Lord Jesus Christ, and thou shalt be saved." Is that it? Yes, that is it! (*3,000 Illustrations for Christian Service*, p. 252).

Dr. Oswald J. Smith illustrates

What It Means to Trust

It was a glorious morning. Great crowds had gathered. The mighty cataract of Niagara thundered on the rocks at the foot of the Falls. A long tightrope stretched from bank to bank, upon which the world's greatest tightrope walker was to cross.

Balancing his long pole lightly, he steps upon the rope and starts across, while the voices of the throngs are hushed, until, as he triumphantly places his foot on the farther bank, a great cheer rises even above the noise of the cataract itself.

Turning to the sea of faces, he now makes a thrilling proposal. He offers to recross the cataract with a man on his back.

But who is to be the man? Excitedly the people talk among themselves.

"Do you believe I am able to carry you across?" at length asks the ropewalker, turning to a likely looking individual.

"I certainly do," at once responds the one addressed.

"Will you let me?" inquires the waiting hero.

"Will I let you? Well, hardly, You don't think I am going to risk my life like that, do you?" and he turns away.

"And what about you?" he asks, as another presents himself.

"I believe. In fact, I have no doubt about it at all."

"Will you trust me?"

"I will!"

Breathlessly the people watch. The pole is balanced; they start; and the great rope tightens beneath their weight. Step by step, slow but sure, without hesitation, they move along. What confidence! The center is reached. They are above the rushing, boiling, foam-covered water, the ugly rocks beneath, poised, as it were, in mid-air.

Now they are nearing the other side. A great hush has fallen on the excited crowds. The people hold their breath. The strain is terrific. At last they are over; the final step is taken, and they stand once more on terra firma, while the spectators go wild with excitement. The tension is broken, the nerve-racking experience ended.

Bridging the gulf between time and eternity is the great rope of salvation. Never yet has it broken. And Jesus Christ along is able to cross it. You may have heard all about it, and, like the first man, you may even believe that Jesus can carry you across. But not until you take the final step and commit yourself to Him will you ever get over. You may believe, but you must trust also.

* * * * *

You are standing on the edge of a great chasm, narrow and deep, spanned by a single plank. Far away in the distance, tearing along at top speed, comes a band of brigands. Unless you cross that plank and reach the other side you are lost.

For some time you hesitate, afraid to take the awful risk, while you examine the plank and think of the fearful precipice below. And while you wait others come running from all directions, and some quickly, some slowly, they cross to the other side.

On come the brigands. You must cross or die! It is a case of "Escape for thy life!"

"What, oh, what shall I do?" you exclaim. "Will the plank hold? True, it holds others. I see scores crossing while I fear and hesitate. Yes, I believe it will hold all right. I believe it will hold me."

Now you have come to the place where you actually "believe" the plank will bear your weight. But are you safe? Are you across? By no means. There must be one more step, there must be "trust," and trust implies action.

At last you grow desperate. You are determined to put it to the test, to act on your intellectual faith. You step on the plank, and in another moment you are over. It has held your weight, and you are safe from your would-be murderers.

My friend, God's great plank of salvation still spans the gulf between earth and Heaven. Millions have already crossed and never yet has it broken. It will hold you, too, if you will but trust.

Oh, yes, you may fully believe that Jesus can save you, but not until you act on that faith and definitely receive Him will you be saved. Will you trust Him? Do it and do it — NOW! (Tract, "What It Means to Trust," Oswald J. Smith).

Dr. L. R. Scarborough gives the two conditions on which men are to escape from the eternal fires of an unending Hell. He says: "All through the records of the Four Gospels it is made plain that the conditions of salvation are two, just two and only two. The minister of the Gospel needs to know this and preach it and teach it everywhere.

1. Repentance from sin. . . .

2. The second great condition of salvation is a personal, voluntary, spiritual acceptance of Jesus Christ as God's substitute for sin. Faith in God's Son is an unalterable condition of salvation. The Bible makes it clear that without it there is no salvation. All through the teachings of Jesus and His apostles this great doctrine appears. . . . On these two terms — repentance from sin towards God, and faith in the Lord Jesus Christ — hangs the destiny of men. Both of these acts must be voluntary. They cannot be forced. No one can perform these acts for another. There is no proxy in religion. Each individual for himself, howsoever wise or howsoever iniquitous, must meet

these terms of life eternal or accept the consequences —
eternal separation from God. . . .

Jesus clearly teaches the following things:

1.   That the unbeliever is condemned already, that he
is under the wrath of God, that he cannot see life, without
faith in the Lord Jesus Christ.

2.   That faith in God's only begotten Son and repentance from sin are the two conditions on which men are to
escape from the eternal fires of an unending hell." (*How
Jesus Won Men*, pp. 199-201, 207. Reprinted by Baker
Book House, 1972).

Christ commands people to "repent ye, and believe the
gospel" (Mark 1:15). God clearly calls sinners to
repentance and faith. "Testifying both to the Jews, and
also to the Greeks, repentance toward God, and faith toward our Lord Jesus Christ" (Acts 20:21).

I realize that man will not and cannot come to God unless God draws him. "No man can come to me, except the
Father which hath sent me draw him: and I will raise him
up at the last day. And he said, Therefore said I unto you,
that no man can come unto me, except it were given unto
him of my Father" (John 6:44,65). In John 12:32 Jesus
stated: "And I, if I be lifted up from the earth, will draw
all men unto me" (John 12:32).

God draws all men, thereby making it possible for all
men to come to Christ and be saved. By God's super-
natural work the sinner is attracted to Christ. In John 1:7
we are told that John the Baptist "came for a witness, to
bear witness of the Light, [Jesus Christ] that all men
through him might believe." God makes it possible for all
men to believe: "will draw *all* men unto me" (John 12:32);
"*all* men through him might believe" (John 1:7).

God also intervenes and makes it possible for a person
to repent. "When they heard these things, they held
their peace, and glorified God, saying, Then hath God
also to the Gentiles *granted repentance unto life*"
(Acts 11:18).

"In meekness instructing those that oppose

themselves; if God peradventure will *give them repentance* to the acknowledging of the truth" (II Timothy 2:25).

The Bible teaches that a person can express his will in rejecting Christ as Saviour and Lord. Jesus said, "And ye will not come to me, that ye might have life" (John 5:40). The only way a sinner could *will not to come* is if he could *will to come*. If he could not have willed to come, then he had no choice in rejecting.

Now to make it clear: every sinner is dead in trespasses and sins, and cannot and will not on his own repent and believe on Christ. God, in His amazing grace, draws all men and gives the sinner the ability to repent and believe on Christ and be saved. When a person is saved, he can look back and realize that he was saved completely by God's grace. If a person dies in his sins and goes to Hell, he must look back and say, "I would not come to Christ and so I have myself to blame. I deserve Hell."

My prayer for every reader of this book is that you will repent and believe on the Lord Jesus Christ and keep out of Hell. Thank God, you don't have to go there. God has given you many warnings and He is not "willing that any should *perish*, but that all should come to repentance" (II Peter 3:9). He promises in John 3:16: "For God so loved the world, that he gave his only begotten Son, that whosoever believeth in him should not *perish*, but have everlasting life." In these two verses God promises that those who repent and believe on the Lord Jesus Christ will not perish (or go to Hell). Come to God today in repentance and faith — there is danger in delay.

Evangelist Sam Jones tells of a man who would not heed the warnings given him concerning a fire and the consequences he suffered:

Fire! Eternal Fire!

In the city of Atlanta, the Wilson House Hotel caught fire some years ago. The servants ran from room to room to awaken the guests. A servant went to one room where

134

there were two men, awakened them. One jumped out of bed, aroused the other, but with a moan and a groan the other man went to sleep again. The guest who was up dressed hurriedly and ran to the bed to shake the other man and said, "Get up, the house is on fire." The other man simply moaned and groaned and went back to sleep. His friend then pulled him out of bed, stood him on his feet and said, "The house is on fire! Hurry, hurry, or you will be burned up!" The man when turned loose fell back into bed with a moan and a groan, and went to sleep again. The next day, as they were raking among the debris of the building, they found his bones all charred and burned. And many a time on earth, Heaven seems to long to arouse us and pull us away from our surroundings and stand us on our feet and cry, "Fire! Eternal Fire!" and yet there we stand, and at last among sulphurous flames and eternal perdition, our bones lie burned and charred forever. (*Preaching Helps: Outlines, Illustrations, and Poems*, Carl G. Johnson, Baker Book House, 1969, p. 27).

Some time ago I read the story of a saloon in Chicago many years ago called "Gates of Hell" which was close to Calvary Church. Someone asked a young man for directions to the "Gates of Hell" saloon, and the young man, in giving directions, said, "Just go right by Calvary and you will come to the 'Gates of Hell'." If you go by Calvary, where Jesus died, and do not receive Him as your personal Saviour, you too will come to the "Gates of Hell" and they will close on you and forever you will be separated from God, and as Dante wrote, you must "abandon all hope, ye who enter here."

I want to close this book with a statement and a prayer of two men who spent their lives in preaching the Gospel so that people could go to Heaven and keep out of Hell.

And now I am come to the conclusion of this work, my heart is troubled to think how I shall leave you; lest after this the flesh should still deceive you, and the world and the devil should keep you asleep and I should leave you as I found you, till you awake in hell. Though in care of your poor souls, I am afraid of this, as knowing the obstinacy of a carnal heart: yet I can say with the prophet Jeremiah, "I have not desired the woeful day, the Lord knoweth." I have not with James and John desired that fire might come from heaven to consume those who refused Jesus Christ. But it is the preventing of the eternal fire that I have been all this while endeavouring: and oh that it had been a needless work! That God and conscience might have been as willing to spare me this labour, as some of you could have been. Dear friends! I am so loth you should lie in everlasting fire, and be shut out of heaven, if it be possible to prevent it, that I shall once more ask you, What do you now resolve? Will you turn or die? (Richard Baxter, *A Call to the Unconverted*, pp. 129-130).

"Father of Spirits, take the heart in hand that is too hard for my weakness. Do not Thou end, though I have done. A word from Thy effectual power will do the work. O Thou, that hast the key of David, that openest and no man shutteth, open Thou this heart, as Thou didst Lydia's, and let the King of Glory enter in, and make this soul Thy captive. Let not the tempter harden him in delays. Let him not stir from this place, nor take his eyes from these lines, till he resolve to forego his sins, and accept life on Thy self-denying terms. In Thy Name, O Lord God, did I go forth to these labours; in Thy name do I close them. Let not all the time they have cost be lost hours; let not all the thoughts of the heart, and all the pains that have been about them be lost labour. Lord, put Thy hand upon the heart of this reader, and send Thy Spirit, as once Thou didst Philip to join himself to the chariot of the eunuch while he was reading the Word. And though I should never know it while I live, yet I beseech Thee, O Lord God, let it be found at the last day that some souls are converted by these labours; and let some be able to stand forth and say that by these persuasions they were won unto Thee. Amen, Amen. Let him that readeth say, Amen." (Joseph Alleine, *Alarm to the Unconverted*, pp. 110-111).

CLOSING APPEAL

I am praying that God will use this book to keep many people out of Hell. I pray that He will use it to keep you out of that awful place. If you want to keep out of Hell you can. Right now, if you are willing to repent and believe on the Lord Jesus Christ, God will save you and you will never go there. Will you do It? If so, pray to God in your own words, or in words similar to these:

"O God, I know that I am a lost sinner and need to be saved from Hell. I want to be saved. Right now, I repent of my sins; I turn from them, and I believe on the Lord Jesus Christ. I believe that He died for my sins, that He rose again and is alive today. I receive Him as my personal Saviour and Lord. I call upon Him to save me. Lord, You said if I would repent of my sins, believe on the Lord Jesus Christ, and call upon Him, You would save me. I believe Your Word: 'For whosoever shall call upon the name of the Lord shall be saved.' I believe You when You say: 'For God so loved the world, that he gave his only begotten Son, that whosoever believeth in him should not perish, but have everlasting life.' Thank You for saving me and giving me everlasting life. In Jesus' Name, Amen."

If you have done this I surely would love to hear from you. I will rejoice with you and will send you a booklet to help you grow in the Christian life.

After you are saved, to be a success as a Christian, you should:

Search the Scriptures daily — Acts 17:11.

Each day you should study the Bible. The word "Success" is mentioned only one time in the Bible (Joshua 1:8), and this verse tells us that we must meditate in the Bible day and night, and then obey it, in order to be a success.

Unceasingly pray — I Thessalonians 5:17.

You should take time to pray every day and often during the day.

Confess Christ — Romans 10:9,10; Matthew 10:32,33; Acts 1:8.

Don't be ashamed of Christ — tell others about Him.

Confess every known sin — I John 1:9.

When you do something that's wrong, immediately confess it to God and He will forgive you.

Enter into the services of a good Bible-preaching church —Hebrews 10:25.

As soon as you are saved, be baptized in water and enter into the fellowship and services of a good Bible-preaching, Bible-loving, and Bible-living church (Acts 2:41,42).

Set aside at least one-tenth of your income for the Lord's work — I Corinthians 16:2; II Corinthians 8:7,8; 9:6,7; Matthew 23:23.

God's people in the Old Testament were commanded to give ten percent to the Lord. We should not give less than that today.

Surrender to the Holy Spirit's working in your life — Ephesians 5:18; Galatians 5:16.

No person can really be a success as God counts success until he is filled or controlled with the Holy Spirit of God. Let Him have His way in your life.

I would appreciate it very much if you would clip out this statement or write it out and send it to me:

Date

Evangelist Carl Johnson
c/o Timothy Books Division
Hearthstone Publications, Inc.
Newtown Ind. Commons
Newtown, Pa. 18940

Dear Brother Johnson:

I have repented and believed on the Lord Jesus Christ and God has saved me. I want you to know this and rejoice with me. I also would like for you to pray for me. Please send me a booklet to help me grow in the Christian life. Thank you.

Signed ....

Address ....

City .... State ....

Zip ....

Bibliography

Alleine, Joseph. *Alarm to the Unconverted.* Evansville, Indiana: Sovereign Grace Publishers, 1959.

Baker, C. J. *The Two Destinies.* Chicago, Illinois: R. Bultmann, n.d.

Bancroft, Emery H. *Christian Theology.* Grand Rapids, Michigan: Zondervan Publishing House, 1961.

Bartlett, Samuel C. *Life and Death Eternal.* Boston: American Tract Society, 1866.

Beecher, Willis Judson. *The Teaching of Jesus Concerning the Future Life.* New York: American Tract Society, 1906.

Biblical Faith of Baptists, The. Detroit, Michigan: Fundamental Baptist Congress of North America, 1964.

Biblical Faith of Baptists, The. Book III. Cincinnati, Ohio: Fundamental Baptist Congress of North America, 1968.

Bibliotheca Sacra. Dallas, Texas: The Faculty of Dallas Theological Seminary and Graduate School of Theology, 1968.

Bunyan, John. *The Strait Gate.* Swengel, Pennsylvania: Reiner Publications, 1967.

Cambron, Mark G. *Bible Doctrines.* Grand Rapids: Zondervan Publishing House, 1954.

Chafer, Lewis Sperry. *Systematic Theology,* Volume 4. Dallas, Texas: Dallas Seminary Press, 1964.

DeHaan, M. R. *After Death . . . What Then?* Grand Rapids: Radio Bible Class, n.d.

———. *Heaven or Hell.* Grand Rapids: Radio Bible Class, n.d.

———. *The Lake of Fire.* Grand Rapids: Radio Bible Class, n.d.

DeHaan, Richard W. *The Eternal Fire*. Grand Rapids: Radio Bible Class, 1968.

Dexter, Henry Martin. *Verdict of Reason*. Boston: Nichols and Noyes, 1865.

Duncan, Homer. *The Lake of Fire*. Lubbock, Texas: Missionary Crusader, n.d.

Evans, William. *The Great Doctrines of the Bible*. Chicago: Moody Press, 1939.

Gordon, S. D. *Quiet Talks About Life After Death*. New York: Fleming H. Revell Company, 1920.

Grant, F. W. *Man and the Future State*. Neptune, New Jersey: Loizeaux Brothers, n.d.

Greene, Oliver P. *Hell*. Greenville, South Carolina: The Gospel Hour, Inc., n.d.

Gunther, Peter F. *Great Sermons by Great Preachers*. Chicago: Moody Press, 1960.

Hoyt, Hermon A. *The End Times*. Chicago: Moody Press, 1969.

Humberd, R. I. *The Lake of Fire*. Flora, Indiana, n.d.

———. *The Last Judgment*. Flora, Indiana, n.d.

Humphrey, J. N. *The Lost Soul's First Day in Eternity*. Chicago: The Christian Witness Company, 1912.

Ironside, H. A. *Death and Afterwards*. Neptune, New Jersey: Loizeaux Brothers, n.d.

———. *Except Ye Repent*. Grand Rapids: Zondervan Publishing House, 1963.

Johnson, Carl G. *Ready for Anything*. Minneapolis, Minnesota: Bethany Fellowship, Inc., 1968.

Knight, Walter B. *3,000 Illustrations for Christian Service*. Grand Rapids: William B. Eerdmans Publishing Company, 1949.

Kuehner, Fred Carl. *Heaven or Hell?*. Washington, D. C.: Christianity Today, n.d.

Landis, Robert W. *The Immortality of the Soul*. New York: Carlton and Porter, 1859.

Lee, Robert G. *Bread from Bellevue Oven*. Murfreesboro, Tennessee: Sword of the Lord Publishers, 1947.

Lockyer, Herbert. *All the Doctrines of the Bible.* Grand Rapids: Zondervan Publishing House, 1964.

———. *Is There A Hell?.* Grand Rapids: Zondervan Publishing House, 1954.

Lowry, Oscar. *Where Are the Dead?.* Chicago: The Bible Institute Colportage Association, 1930.

Macartney, Clarence Edward. *Putting on Immortality.* Old Tappan, New Jersey: Fleming H. Revell Company, 1926.

McCrossan, T. J. *The Bible: Its Hell and Its Ages.* Seattle, Washington: T. J. McCrossan, 1941.

Merrill, S. M. *The New Testament Idea of Hell.* Cincinnati, Ohio: Hitchcock & Walden, 1878.

Miller, H. S. *The Christian Workers' Manual.* Harrisburg, Pennsylvania: Christian Alliance Publishing Company, 1928.

Mundell, George H. *The Destiny of A Lost Soul.* Fort Washington, Pennsylvania: Christian Literature Crusade, 1969.

Munsey, William Elbert. *Eternal Retribution!* Murfreesboro, Tennessee: Sword of the Lord Publishers, 1951.

Myers, John. *Voices from the Edge of Eternity.* Northridge, California: Voice Publications, 1968.

Nave, Orvil J. *Nave's Topical Bible.* Chicago: Moody Press, n.d.

Newell, William R. *Romans Verse by Verse.* Chicago: Grace Publications, 1945.

North, Brownlow. *The Rich Man and Lazarus.* Banner of Truth Trust, 1961.

Orr, William W. *The Tragedy of Hell and How to Escape It.* Wheaton, Illinois: Scripture Press Publications, Inc., 1968.

Other Room. New York: The Macmillan Company, 1904.

Pache, Rene. *The Future Life.* Chicago: Moody Press, 1962.

Pentecost, J. Dwight. *Things to Come.* Grand Rapids: Dunham Publishing Company, 1958.

——. *Things Which Become Sound Doctrine*. Grand Rapids: Zondervan Publishing House, 1969.

Pink, Arthur W. *The Attributes of God*. Swengel, Pennsylvania: Reiner Publications, n.d.

Rice, John R. *Hell! What the Bible Says About It*. Murfreesboro, Tennessee: Sword of the Lord Publishers, 1942.

——. *Soul-Saving Sermons*. *Murfreesboro, Tennessee:* Sword of the Lord Publishers, 1963.

——. *Twelve Tremendous Themes*. Murfreesboro, Tennessee: Sword of the Lord Publishers, 1943.

Ridenour, Fritz. *So, What's the Difference?* Glendale, California: Gospel Light Publications, 1967.

Rimmer, Harry. *The Evidences for Immortality*. Berne, Indiana: The Berne Witness Company, 1945.

Roberson, Lee. *Death . . . and After?* Chattanooga, Tennessee: Lee Roberson, 1954.

Robertson, Irvine. *What the Cults Believe*. Chicago: Moody Press, 1966.

Ryrie, Charles Caldwell. *A Survey of Bible Doctrine*. Chicago: Moody Press, 1972.

Sabiers, Karl. *Where Are the Dead?* Los Angeles, California: Christian Pocket Books, 1959.

Sanders, J. Oswald. *Heresies and Cults*. London: Marshall, Morgan & Scott, 1948.

Scarborough, L. R. *Prepare to Meet God*. Grand Rapids: Baker Book House, 1971.

Seiss, J. A. *The Apocalypse*. Grand Rapids: Zondervan Publishing House, n.d.

Smith, Oswald J. *Atheism and the Bible*. Chicago: The Moody Bible Institute, 1937.

——. *Man's Future Destiny*. Grand Rapids: Zondervan Publishing House, 1940.

——. *The Message of Hope*. London: Marshall, Morgan & Scott, 1963.

Stover, Ross H. *What Do We Know About Life After Death?* Grand Rapids: Zondervan Publishing House, 1941.

Swedenborg, Emanuel. *Heaven and Its Wonders and Hell.* Philadelphia: J. P. Lippincott and Company, 1876.

Spencer, Duane Edward. *The Key Word Hell.* n.d.

Strauss, Lehman. *An Examination of the Doctrine of Jehovah's Witnesses.* New York: Loizeaux Brothers, 1942.

———. *Life After Death.* Westchester, Illinois: Good News Publishers, 1961.

Sumner, Robert L. *Hell Is No Joke.* Murfreesboro, Tennessee: Sword of the Lord Publishers, 1959.

Thomas, F. W. *Masters of Deception.* Grand Rapids: Baker Book House, n.d.

Torrey, R. A. *Real Salvation.* New York: Fleming H. Revell Company, 1905.

———. *What the Bible Teaches.* Ol Tappan, New Jersey: Fleming H. Revell Company, 1898.

Townsend, L. T. *Lost Forever.* New York: Lee and Shepard, 1874.

Van Baalen, Jan Karel. *The Chaos of Cults.* Grand Rapids: William B. Eerdmans Publishing Company, 1938, 1951, 1956.

Vine, W. E. *Expository Dictionary of New Testament Words.* Westwood, New Jersey: Fleming H. Revell Company, 1940.

Walvoord, John F. *The Revelation of Jesus Christ.* Chicago: Moody Press, 1966.

Watts, Isaac. *The End of Time.* Dayton, Ohio: More, Clarke & Company, 1854.

Wuest, Kenneth S. *Wuest's Word Studies from the Greek New Testament,* Volume 3. Grand Rapids: William B. Eerdmans Publishing Company, 1966.

Woodson, Leslie H. *Hell and Salvation.* Old Tappan, New Jersey: Fleming H. Revell Company, 1973.

10 more

popular inspirational paperbacks from timothy books

1 **Demons, the Bible and You**—An anthology on the occult by Russell T. Hitt, J. Stafford Wright, William J. Peterson and other authorities on demonology and satanism.

2 **Your God and Your Gold** (Leslie B. Flynn)—A reminder to our materialistic culture of our stewardship responsibility.

3 **Hell, You Say**—Carl Johnson, well-known author and evangelist, analyzes the biblical view of hell

4 **Health, Wealth and Happiness** (Dr. Ralph W. Neighbour, Sr.)— Solomon's key to successful living, from the book of Proverbs.

5 **Set Free** (Addison C. Raws)—Seventeen men whose lives prove that no alcoholic needs to despair.

6 **Go, Christian, Go**—A primer on successful Christian living by William S. Deal.

7 **It's About Time**—Dr. Leslie Flynn discusses man's most valuable resource and how to make the most of it.

8 **A Merry Heart**—A storehouse of humor for speakers and masters of ceremonies, from toastmaster Dr. Russell Pavy.

9 **On Our Way Rejoicing** (Ingrid Trobisch)—The incredible saga of a great missionary family.

10 **They Looked for a City** (Lydia Buksbazen)—The gripping true story of a Jewish family and their bitter but triumphant struggle for survival.

Available from your Christian bookstore or

timothy books

Newtown Industrial Commons
Newtown, PA 18940